What readers are saying about
Sell Your Home *FASTER* with Feng Shui

"Sell Your Home Faster with Feng Shui is flying off our shelves! We're delighted to be carrying your book."

Tracie Mertz, California Department of Real Estate

"I love your book and have used it for a workshop teaching real estate professionals. The copies I had sold in a flash and I'd like to order more to have on hand. Thanks for doing such wonderful work!"

G. vanZon, Ponte Dedra Beach, Florida

"My daughter used your book and sold her house in seven days... a miracle in the Denver market. Thanks so much!"

D. Condra, Aurora, Colorado

"I liked the clarity and simplicity of your approach ... your book made a difficult subject understandable with clear examples of how the seller benefits financially by applying Feng Shui principles."

J. Wawro, San Luis Obispo, California

"We want to share our good news with you: After reading your book we put our home up for sale and in less than a month we will be closing escrow. Your book was so helpful and informative."

J. Streltzer, Kansas City, Missouri

"When will your book, Buy Real Estate SMARTER with Feng Shui, be available? I have gotten so much value from your first book."

P. Traynor, Chicago, Illinois

"Your book is invaluable to those trying to sell their homes and also great for real estate agents to give to their clients... I highly recommend it."

N. Singleton, Vancouver, Canada

"I was so impressed with your book I gave my REALTOR a copy. He was particularly enthusiastic and said (your book) is the best Feng Shui reference guide he has for real estate professionals and homeowners alike."

S. Kobacker, Santa Barbara, California

Also Available at Your Favorite Bookstore

Feng Shui Your Workspace for Dummies

Holly Ziegler with Jennifer Lawler
Wiley Publishing

Other Holly Ziegler Titles Available Soon

Buy Real Estate SMARTER with Feng Shui
Ancient Secrets to Analyze and Select Property Wisely

100 Feng Shui Tips to Sell Your Home Faster
A Pocket Guide of Ancient Secrets To Make Buyers Want YOUR House

100 Feng Shui Tips to Buy Real Estate Smarter
A Pocket Guide of Ancient Secrets To Choose Property Wisely

Feng Shui in the Classroom
Ancient Wisdom to Empower Teachers and Produce Smarter Students

Feng Shui Week by Week
52 Articles to Guide Your Tranquil Path Through the Seasons

Dragon Chi™ Publications

Sell Your Home
FASTER
with Feng Shui

Sell Your Home
FASTER
with Feng Shui

Ancient Wisdom to
Expedite the Sale of Real Estate

by
Holly Ziegler, MA. Ed.

Dragon Chi™ Publications
Arroyo Grande, California

Sell Your Home FASTER with Feng Shui
Ancient Wisdom to Expedite the Sale of Real Estate
by Holly Ziegler

Published by: **Dragon Chi™ Publications**
Post Office Box 1036 • Arroyo Grande, CA 93421

Foreword by His Holiness Grand Master Professor Lin Yun, Ph.D.
Preface by Jami Lin
Edited by Arlene Winn, Melody DeMeritt and
the Cal Poly Tech Writing students, Spring, 2001.
Feng Shui editing by Jami Lin
Illustrations by Gini Griffin, Francine Van De Vanter, Jim Ross, and Holly Ziegler.
Formatting by Kerry Randall and Jacquie Blanquies
Original Chinese paper cuts from Yangchow were used for many of the graphics.
Grateful acknowledgement is made to Terah Kathryn Collins and Hay House Publishing
Co. for the use of the graphic of the Five Elements and to Lillian Too and Konsep
Books for the use of the Luo-Pan graphic.

The purpose of this book is to educate and inform. The intent of the author is to offer information of a general nature to assist the reader toward the goal of selling their house. The author does not assume any responsibility for situations that people allege to have been produced by the interpretation or use of any information contained in this book, directly or indirectly.
Printed in the United States of America

ISBN 0 – 9710652 – 8 – 4   (pbk.)

Library of Congress Control Number: 2001117568

Acknowledgements

An enormous debt of gratitude is owed to the many people who helped make this book a reality, both in real estate, and in the field of feng shui. I feel *especially blessed* to have worked with the real estate firm of Mallory-Berryhill for nearly twenty-five years. I have had as my brokers Jack Mallory and Terry Berryhill, the two finest teacher-mentors an agent could ask for. Their unwavering insistence on the highest and most ethical standards in the business, as well as their constant support and great sense of humor, pulled me through even the worst of days. *Thanks to them, after all these years, I still love selling real estate.* I am most grateful to my family of fellow-agents at Mallory-Berryhill, who encouraged me throughout this project and kept the feng shui fountain on my desk constantly filled with water!

And to the following:

Anne Rice, who from college roommate days always opened the finest inspirational doors for me, for first introducing me to the exciting world of feng shui.

Karin Leonard, my spiritual sister, for her love and openhearted guidance over the years, and for always encouraging me to step into my higher self. Her selfless and creative spirit has nurtured mine, and when I need her most, she is there.

Arlene Winn, my friend and editor, for her wondrous sense of humor as well as her tireless efforts to keep me succinct. Working with her on this project has kept me both silly and sane… she is such a gift in my life.

Duane Waddell for his endearing support and wisdom during the many long hours I spent with my laptop computer.

Kerry Randall, my outstanding formatting wizard who took a lump of clay and turned it into a work of art.

Robert J. Bruss, esteemed real estate attorney, broker, educator, syndicated columnist, and prolific author *par excellance*, for his awesome information and up-to-the-minute legal advice.

David Daniel Kennedy for his assistance with decisions about content and wording... for being available to me, despite a busy schedule, with exceptional feng shui knowledge, insight, and focus.

Terah Kathryn Collins, whose ***Western Guide to Feng Shui***, is a text I use in teaching my college courses... for her clarity and inspirational combination of practical feng shui with beautiful spiritual insights.

James Moser for his dedication and energy in sharing the world of feng shui with others, and especially for the outstanding courses I took from him early on in my feng shui path. Thanks to him I recognized the force of this design-science and understood its unique possibilities in the realm of real estate.

William Spear, whose great book ***Feng Shui Made Easy***, did exactly that. His excellent work demystified my questions and illustrated the power of this amazing eco-art.

Stephen Skinner for his continuing contribution to furthering world-wide knowledge of feng shui, and whose highly instructive book, ***The Living Earth Manual of Feng Shui***, was where my study began. His excellent work both fascinated and intrigued me — I've been hooked ever since.

Jami Lin, dear fellow China-adventurer, for her inspiration, wisdom, and boundless energy. Such a giver, and one of my favorite people… her literary contributions to the world of feng shui are among my favorites. To know Jami is to love her.

Helen and James Jay, who twice unlocked the beauty and feng shui mysteries of China for me; and whose quiet, smiling, and gentle spirits make arduous and challenging journeys a pure delight. I am so grateful that you both have come into my feng shui world.

Denise Linn, gifted author, speaker, and teacher who so unselfishly gave me her time and excellent suggestions, in order that this work serve my readers in the highest way. It is my privilege and delight to have your assistance.

Lillian Too, the highly respected First Lady of feng shui, who has led countless students, I among them, into this magical world through her many excellent books. Learning directly in a class from Lillian is a gift — punctuated with laughter, her desire to be in humble service to others, and deep knowledge.

And especially to His Holiness Grand Master, Professor Thomas Lin Yun, whose inspirational teaching, generosity, and selfless sharing of feng shui wisdom have lifted my spirits and raised my chi more than I thought possible.

…and to the many others, not specifically mentioned here, who have given me such valuable assistance and support in countless ways, I am so grateful.

Dedication

To my dearest mother, Nana,

whose example throughout my life,

has made all the difference;

and to Jonathan and Jacqueline who bring me such joy.

Chinese proverb…

When there is light in the soul,
there is beauty in the person.

When there is beauty in the person,
there is harmony in the home.

When there is harmony in the home,
there is honor in the nation.

When there is honor in the nation,
there is peace in the world.

Table of Contents

Appendices

Foreword

H. H. Feng Shui Grandmaster Professor Lin Yun, Ph.D.

It is difficult enough to write a book, and it is even more difficult to write a good book about Feng Shui. To write a book with the main purpose of speeding up the transaction of selling your house using various Feng Shui techniques has got to be the most difficult of all. Therefore, I am very happy to see this new, one-of-a-kind book, *Sell Your Home FASTER with Feng Shui,* by Holly Ziegler.

The main points of this book deal with the specific study of selling the house using the power of Feng Shui. The book begins with an emphasis on the interior design of the home, showing how to dress up the front entryway, the deck, patio, landscaping, and skillfully showing the property to its best advantage.

Further, by using the techniques Holly describes, the smart seller will be able to find the best and most diligent real estate agent who hopefully has some Feng Shui knowledge! A careful reading of *Sell Your Home FASTER with Feng Shui,* will enable the seller and the listing broker to thoroughly understand how to present and introduce the house's positive points and thereby maximize its value.

As for selling a home with speed and smoothly completing the transaction, *Sell Your Home FASTER with Feng Shui* presents a variety of case studies that illustrate actual success stories using these principles. Also one will find the *I-Ching* Trigrams and Feng Shui Bagua. The ever-thoughtful author also teaches many Black Sect Tantric Buddhist transcendental solutions which not only solve problems but speed up the eventual sale. Most notably, the author goes a step further and includes a thorough index, as well as introduces useful Feng Shui terminology, and recommendations for further reading, all of which add tremendous value to this book.

It is for all these reasons that I have said this book is indeed one-of-a-kind, and readers will receive great benefits by carefully studying and putting into practice its suggestions. *Unexpected and positive results will be achieved in selling a property... as long as you do your part as a seller, both you and the buyer, as well as the real estate agents, will achieve a win-win transaction.* This is gaining many advantages with a single move. Because of this, the author of *Sell Your Home FASTER with Feng Shui* has accumulated much good karma without knowing it. This is another reason I take delight in writing the foreword for this book by Holly Ziegler.

Lin Yun
Feng Shui Grand Master
Berkeley, California
October, 2000

*Grand Master Thomas Lin Yun, a worldwide leading authority on feng shui, and an **I Ching** scholar, is the founder and spiritual leader of contemporary Black Sect Tantric Buddhism.*

He can be contacted through:
Yun Lin Temple
2959 Russell Street
Berkeley, CA 94705.
Tel: (510) 841-2347 • Fax: (510) 548-2621

Preface

By Jami Lin

As an interior designer and Feng Shui practitioner for many years, I helped many people sell their homes with the principles outlined in Holly's well-written book. Without a doubt, Feng Shui helps sell property! The best part of *Sell Your Home FASTER with Feng Shui* is that it can be read easily; your valuable time can be spent preparing your home to close and you can rest assured you will receive the highest market value.

Holly's priceless quips ("raise the chi and raise the value") and step-by-step instructions make the often-difficult processes of selling a home and moving, seamless and joyful. As you prepare your house to sell, she describes the essentials of what to donate, which treasures to pre-pack so you can help the buyer remember your home (and not all the stuff.). She then explains the valuable do's and don'ts of working with qualified brokers, how inspections are handled, and the complex legalities involved in selling real estate. Her numerous checklists will provide invaluable help as you move through the selling process.

She reminds you that while location is vital, it is likely your home is one of several for sale in the neighborhood. Holly shows you how to win the buyers' hearts. Price is always a factor, but what is it that will make a buyer want to purchase your home instead of one a few blocks away? Holly shares the most important aspects of a buyer's decision-making process so your home gets purchased, fast! Prospective new owners want their new property to enhance their life, and when they walk through your front door and into each room, they want to feel as though they are already home.

A home is like a mirror, a reflection of you. Holly shows you how to make your house irresistible. Using the simplicity of Feng Shui, potential buyers can visualize how their furniture, their accessories, and their life will be when they buy your property. Her information will help your house speak to its new owner: "You will love coming home, cooking in the kitchen, watching the kids play in the yard, and helping them with their homework in the study. You'll love waking up every day in the sumptuous bedroom and taking a bubble in the tub." Whatever your home's charms and qualities, Holly helps you prepare it so buyers can visualize themselves living there… and loving it.

Feng Shui is extremely useful in its capacity to harness earth energy and heaven energy to maximize life potential. In the process of buying and selling a house, Holly describes the magical moment when a buyer feels they have *come home*. From personally experiencing the magic moment (even though there was no question that my dream home needed extensive work), the moment I walked in, I knew I had finally come home, and I started to cry tears of joy. (One thing Holly didn't mention: When a prospective buyer cries, you get your asking price!)

Holly has made it easy to sell your house with Feng Shui. Now, how do you *buy* a house that feels like home? one that will energetically support and nurture both you and your loved ones in all aspects of your lives? Rumor has it that she is working on a new book, *Buy Your Home SMARTER with Feng Shui.* And that's a good thing since there are few things more important to all aspects of your life than having a home with good Feng Shui!

Jami Lin is an internationally recognized feng shui lecturer and consultant. She is the author of three best selling feng shui titles: **Feng Shui Today: Earth Design - The Added Dimension; The Feng Shui Anthology;** *and* **The Essence of Feng Shui.**

Introduction

The purpose of this book is to help you get your house sold. Homes with good feng shui (pronounced *fung schway*) sell *faster*. I can say with certainty that dwellings where age-old methods of bringing harmony, balance, order, and simple beauty are used, *appeal* to buyers. I base this conviction on both my 25 year background as a highly successful real estate broker on California's Central Coast, and my intensive study of feng shui in China and in the United States with recognized masters since 1994.

Feng shui, an eco-science of intentional design and serenity that originated in China about four thousand years ago, is having a resurgence in popularity for very practical reasons — it works. Think of feng shui as *environmental space therapy*™. If you are considering putting your house on the market, or if you have tried unsuccessfully to sell your house, feng shui methods can be exactly what you need to get the job done — quickly! Just as treatments applied in medical disciplines use a physical remedy to cure a disease or other disorder, feng shui principles can be a cure for what ails your home.

In a real estate sense, feng shui is just what the doctor ordered because this design science is about making a house *feel good* to buyers. *Rid your home of what is troublesome or uncomfortable, and it becomes more saleable.* I've seen how my own listings sell faster when the owners apply the feng shui techniques I suggest — buyers immediately like what they see and feel. Today, more than ever before, home buyers seek not only a roof over their heads, but a dwelling that gives them a serene and healing space, a comfortable nest away from the stress and frantic energy of the outside world. When you manifest and create those healing qualities in your home, buyers respond.

This book is filled with practical advice from the world of real estate as well as the time-tested, environmental design philosophy of feng shui. It blends both domains — modern savvy and ancient wisdom — that is the *winning combination* for marketing your home.

Sell Your Home FASTER with Feng Shui is divided into three sections:

- **Section I: Tools for Seekers** - For those readers wanting background information about feng shui, its origins, history, and information
- **Section II: Tools for Change** - Feng shui tips and guidelines to put to use right away to sell your home.
- **Section III: Tools of the Trade** - Real estate knowledge and specific information to help you through the business side of the selling transaction.

Using feng shui techniques is not necessarily about spending a lot of money or re-locating the position of your front door. You are going to need creativity, discipline, a bit of hard work, and the ability to seriously consider new and fresh ideas. The more you are willing to apply these principles, the faster you'll see that SOLD sign in your front yard. Relatively speaking, your home will be in escrow quicker than you can say "feng shui!"

Have an open mind, decide to roll up your sleeves, and enjoy the process of becoming a feng shui - real estate success story!

Holly Ziegler

Section I

Tools for Seekers...

Learn Feng Shui History and Basics

Origins of Feng Shui

"The five essential factors that determine the quality of one's life: first comes destiny, then comes luck... third is feng shui, then right action, and education..."

— Chinese Proverb

Shirley had been trying to sell her house for five months. An executive with a busy schedule, she had little time to focus on anything more than her intensive workload and making sure she still had room in the day for her teenage daughter. Her house was older and small, but in an excellent neighborhood and close to a good school. She felt that Colleen, her agent, was working hard on her listing, but when buyers came to a showing, they did not come back a second time.

Frustrated by a lack of interested buyers, Shirley had already lowered her price. Then her friend told her about a book she had read on feng shui, and how some of the ideas of this Eastern art of placement might give her a fresh approach to getting her house sold. Shirley read her friend's book and decided immediately to make some feng shui adjustments in her home.

Following the book's suggestions, and willing to give anything a try, Shirley put a large mirror on the wall in the very small, dark entryway and kept a simple vase of fresh flowers on the plant stand in the corner. Outside, next to the front porch, she installed a fountain and made sure the flowing water was moving toward the entry. She planted colorful new flowers along the front pathway and repainted the forlorn-looking front door.

Beginning to feel a definite difference in the house, Shirley raised the blinds she normally kept closed during the day and made sure a few windows were always open for fresh air. She asked for her daughter's help with keeping the toilet lid down and the bathroom door closed. Finally, she set a powerful intention: she was determined to get her house sold and she was ready to welcome the buyer who would love and enjoy her home.

After two weeks, Shirley noticed several potential buyers had come back for a second tour of her home. The following day Colleen called and told her that an agent would bring an offer to the office that afternoon. After a brief negotiation, Shirley happily signed an acceptable bid from a young couple that felt her house was perfect for them.

Living in Serenity

Feng shui, pronounced *fung schway,* and translates literally from Chinese as "wind and water," the two universal forces that sustain life; it is the ancient philosophy of harmonious placement and balance within a space. Defined somewhere between an art and a science, its goal is to bring balance, blessings, abundance, and tranquility into a particular area and to those who dwell within it. Feng shui is about living in harmony with our environment and *emphasizing our fundamental connection with nature.* This idea may be somewhat new in the West, but in the East, the concept of intentionally seeking compatibility with one's living space is very old.

A philosophy that blends simple wisdom with the practicality of careful planning and observation, feng shui can be practiced on a city lot, on a large rural piece of land, within a home, in an office setting, and in large commercial buildings such as banks, hotels and convention centers. Its principles can be applied in a big city or on a small desktop; it literally knows no bounds and has no boundaries.

Feng shui is the age-old Chinese design science that balances the natural and material realms, bringing tranquility and harmony into a living space. Here we find a serene environment where homes *feel* good and have a peaceful essence so necessary to our human comfort zones. As if receiving a therapy of sorts, buyers experience a positive inward response to houses with good feng shui. In their mind's eye, buyers like what they see and enjoy what they feel while in a space that has good feng shui.

Sellers who follow feng shui guidelines usually get quick results, and this book is intended to give you the information you need to implement its methods to sell your home faster. If you use these principles, your property will stand out in the mind of the buyer as being an excellent choice. Not only do these ancient concepts work to sell property, feng shui can be creative and fun — even if you are not trying to sell your house!

Buyers are very discriminating; they shop around and look at many houses before making a final decision. Knowing this and realizing that the real estate competition can be very stiff, the smart seller will appeal to buyers in as many ways as possible, including the often-subtle design techniques of feng shui. This approach to marketing a property insures that their particular product will remain in the buyer's consciousness long after the initial showing.

Owners with this in mind work to create a lasting and positive *impression,* rather than merely a physical space. Consequently, the buyer retains that wondrous image in a visual as well as in an intrinsic, internal way. They leave the premises feeling happy and satisfied as if they have had a wonderful meal. Feng shui provides the perfect recipe for this delectable real estate delight. In a way, you might say that feng shui feeds the soul.

Taking this idea a few steps further, Jami Lin in her book *Feng Shui Today: Earth Design, the Added Dimension,* explains, "The Chinese understood that by designing our spaces within the harmony of the natural laws and by bringing them inside, we feed our souls. When our souls are well fed, we are more sensitive and make better decisions. The greater our awareness, the greater is the potential of fulfilling our dreams. The more that is shared, the more that comes back." [1] In other words, buyers want their dreams fulfilled and feng shui is here to help you.

The first three chapters of *Sell Your Home FASTER with Feng Shui* are intended for those readers who want more in-depth information about this environmental design science of harmony and balance. Section I introduces the origins and basic principles of feng shui. However, realizing that not everyone who needs to sell their home will feel compelled to study feng shui fundamentals, this initial section can be skipped if the reader chooses. Many excellent volumes

---

[1] *Feng Shui Today: Earth Design, the Added Dimension,* Jami Lin, Earth Design, Inc., p. 13.

are already available in bookstores to those wanting to study feng shui even further.

Ancient Wisdom for Modern Times

Donald Trump not only insisted that feng shui experts guide him in designing the Trump Towers, but it is reported that he employs them on all of his real estate projects. When the managers of the new Denver Airport had major difficulties starting operations, and after they had tried everything else, they decided to call in feng shui consultants. Soon the airport was up and running. The Esprit™ Corporation in San Francisco recently had their new offices feng shui-ed to ensure a more harmonious work environment and to boost productivity and profits. A large development corporation in the San Jose, California, area called in a feng shui professional to assess the site for hundreds of homes and to provide insight about the ideal location before breaking ground.

In an effort to understand and comply with the desires of their clients, real estate brokers, especially in larger cosmopolitan areas, are more frequently seeking out the advice of feng shui experts. They wish to honor the numerous requests from Asian buyers and from everyday home-seekers from all backgrounds. Feng shui may not be mainstream real estate practice yet, but it is well on its way.

Brokers and agents paying attention to this wisdom of the ancients also find that feng shui is greatly based on old-fashioned common sense. When it comes to siting homes and enhancing what will raise the *chi* or good energy of a particular piece of property, feng shui guidelines from thousands of years ago show that what worked then can be used with confidence today. *The bottom line is results —* the property sells.

Putting the Power of Feng Shui to Work

Although applying feng shui principles will give you a definite advantage in selling your home, understanding some of the reasons many Chinese (and other Asians) make the choices they do will give you an insight into *why and how* the eco-science of feng shui has been used so successfully.

We may ask, why do Asian buyers pay special attention to the properties that surround the one they wish to buy, the position of the home on the street, and how the house sits in relation to other dwellings? Why are they particularly careful about kitchen and bathroom placement, and avoid houses where the stairway to a second level is directly opposite the front door? For what reason is it important for the followers of feng shui to select dwellings where the master bedroom is in the southwest and preferably right rear corner of the house?

Sell Your Home FASTER with Feng Shui answers these questions and many more. It provides you with useful tips for selling your home to *all buyers*, whether or not they are familiar with feng shui. You are encouraged to unlock your creativity and be inspired as you peer through this ancient design lens. If you keep an open mind, you will not only sell your home faster, you will have a good time in the process.

A Tune Up for Your Home

We have all been in homes where we felt very comfortable and wanted to stay for a long time. We have also been in houses where we had an uneasy feeling and couldn't leave fast enough. Just like a quality mechanic tunes up our cars to make them run more easily, or a chiropractor gives our bodies a thorough adjustment to make our muscles and bones feel better, feng shui does the same thing with the energy or chi in our homes. On a subtle, yet very real level, we like what we see as well as what we feel — we feel at home.

With feng shui, we deal with what some refer to as the *energetic atmosphere* of a home. When we live in this subconscious ambience of serenity, we are more healthy, efficient, and successful in

9

our daily lives. This quality, or essence, is about how a space affects our moods and our internal comfort zone; it determines whether we wish to linger or leave. Chiropractors work with our skeletal anatomy; feng shui works with our home's energetic or subtle anatomy.

Applying feng shui to the sale of real estate, the logic follows that when a property has the quality of feeling good to a buyer, they will want to spend more time there, bond emotionally with the house, and imagine that they can live comfortably within that particular space. They envision their own furniture in place; they actually think about having meals at their table in this particular kitchen or dining area and placing their bed in the master bedroom. They picture their children playing in the yard and having their friends over for a barbecue. As the buyer relaxes into this stage of delightful, yet serious dreaming, an offer to purchase is often the next step.

The Beauty and Blessings from Nature

Feng shui has always been tied to the land, and the ancient Chinese venerated the landscape. Their early philosophy, poetry, and art reflected a cultural desire to identify with the beauty and balance they found in the natural world. They believed it was not wise to go against nature's course, or to cause man-made upheaval by seriously disrupting what nature had already put in place. They felt that actions such as this would ultimately hurt man and bring him misfortune. So when building a city, temple, road, home, or farm, they took great pains to avoid disturbing the earth's flesh. [2]

---

[2] *Interior Design with Feng Shui,* Sarah Rossbach, p.7.

10

Feng shui principles showed the ancient Chinese that they should work with natural earth contours and land formations as they implemented their architectural designs and constructed their buildings. It emphasizes the compatibility of man with nature and how best to achieve the perfect union of both. The land itself and Mother Earth are considered to be almost sacred — clear streams and waterways are prized, trees and foliage are protected and preserved wherever possible, and close attention is paid to treating the natural terrain with great respect.

In China, it has long been understood that we are powerfully affected by our surroundings; our innermost selves react in a direct way to the spaces we occupy. If our environment is cluttered, unclean, messy, disorganized, or crowded we find it difficult to relax and find serenity within this space. On the other hand, if our setting is uncluttered, clean, organized, and allowed to be more spacious, our mind and spirit feel calmer, or grounded, and we are more readily able to savor the beauty and blessings in our lives.

Grave Beginnings

Originally called *Kan Yu*, feng shui was first used in the ancient Orient for determining the most auspicious location for graves. The idea was that if one's ancestors were resting happily in an ideally located place, they would bless and bestow good fortune on their earthly family. The Chinese believe that we have a direct connection with our predecessors, and that they are *present* in a spiritual sense guiding and directing their loved ones still on this physical plane. To revere the dearly departed is wise as well as respectful; furthermore, it is well advised not to tempt fate.

The Chinese made special efforts to find the ideal site where gentle breezes and richness of the land would ensure an auspicious and comfortable resting place for the honored ancestor. Feng shui provided the information that helped determine ideal burial sites where the entrance always faced south into the warmth of the sun and whose back braced against the strong winds and stormy weather coming from the north. The elaborate series of Ming Tombs built during the 14th and 15th centuries outside Beijing are excellent examples of feng shui used for imperial burials. [3]

Reading the Land

To survive and prosper, the Chinese would call upon early feng shui masters to assess the energy or chi they felt was inherent in the ground. These geomancy experts were expected to be pure in spirit and intention and were highly respected for their knowledge of the earth and wisdom about nature. Passed down from master to pupil, the secrets of reading the land were associated with observing the rolling of the hills, the undulations of earth energy in mountains and valleys, and the symbolic shapes seen in land formations. Somewhat like water dowsers of today, they examined the landscape and gave advice about where best to place a grave, build a house, or position a city.

These experts would determine exactly where the forces of nature were not too harsh, nor in conflict with any strong elements

---

[3] *The Wisdom of China and India,* Lin Yuatang, p.1104.

such as watercourses or erosion. They would calculate the best position where the heavenly and terrestrial elements were aligned. They paid close attention to clues in the landscape and looked for signs of auspicious natural elements or qualities, such as vibrant plant life, healthy animals, sweet water, balmy breezes, and rich soil. Sites with jagged or unusually shaped rock outcroppings, dry watercourses, sparse vegetation, dying or unhealthy animals, and harsh winds were avoided as potential building locations. Using these methods, slowly over time, early feng shui developed into the environmental wisdom and design science we have today. [4]

Raise the *Chi*... Increase the Value

Good feng shui has the potential to up the energetic ante of a property, which delights both the senses and the soul. It will also raise the market appeal and, therefore, raise the real estate value. In ancient times, as well as today, it was understood that the magic of a good location pays wondrous dividends for the enjoyment of the occupants, as well as making it a highly desirable property to pass along later to a new owner at an appreciated price!

Besides location, *sellers need to realize that the ambience of a home or property is all-important to buyers.* When the atmosphere of a house is brought into feng shui alignment, the level of desirability is raised; it is closer to being called a home — a dwelling that is lived in, enjoyed, and treasured. Allowing the inherent inner beauty in each

---

[4] *Feng Shui for Beginners,* Richard Webster, pp. 21-24.

piece of property to shine with its own positive, energetic essence, no matter how humble or how lavish, is the goal of feng shui.

This work is about much more than just rearranging furniture. Understanding that the positive results are endless, this design science shows us how to achieve this exceptionally desirable quality within our homes and more importantly *why* to do it. The reward is living more comfortably and intentionally, and finding the inner tranquility we seek within our sacred space.

Feng shui originated with the emperor and the ruling class, and later filtered down to the common people. The wealthy and educated sensed the power it gave them and they enjoyed the luxury of being able to relocate or rebuild if the feng shui wasn't just right. It was understood that the advantages of good feng shui far outweighed the financial expenditure to make needed corrections. In modern times, cures or solutions are put in place when design challenges arise within a space because few people have the ability to move or remodel due to questionable feng shui.

Just as the lovely mist that moves around Chinese mountaintops is thought to bring fortunate blessings, similarly, it is believed that good feng shui on your side will tip the scales of fortune in your favor. It was felt from early times that this somewhat mysterious art of wind and water cooperated with and harnessed the universal energy of chi within a space, thus bringing overall well-being and abundance to those who followed its philosophy. This insight of deriving both tangible as well as non-tangible benefits from feng shui is being revived today at a healthy rate.

It All Began with the Emperor and the Tortoise

Legend has it that feng shui originated in approximately 2900 B.C. with the Emperor Fu Hsi who some consider to be the father of Chinese civilization. As the story goes, while he sat meditating on the bank of the Yangtze River, a giant tortoise emerged from the water and came to rest nearby. In a state of profound inspiration, Fu Hsi saw upon the tortoise the orderly lined markings of the shell, which turned out to be the pattern for the numbers found within the lo-shu or Magic Square. The marking sequence was further developed by Fu Hsi into the trigrams of the *I Ching*, or ***The Book of Changes***.

The unique mathematical construct of the Magic Square is arranged in such a way that all the numbers from one through nine add up to fifteen in any direction. Along with scientific observations of planetary movement and astronomy, this Magic Square became the foundation for Chinese numerology, astrology, the construct of the Nine Star *Ki*, and eventually feng shui. [5]

4	9	2
3	5	7
8	1	6

The Lo Shu Numbers of the Magic Square

---

[5] Ibid, p. 77.

Ancient Wisdom of the *I Ching*

The *I Ching* is considered to be the oldest book in China and is said to be the only Confucian text to survive the great Burning of Books in 215 B.C. Also referred to as *The Book of Changes,* it is believed to contain the secrets of life and has had an incalculable effect on Chinese culture, philosophy, and fundamental thinking about life. [6] The book is still widely read and consulted by philosophers and students of Eastern thought. Its wisdom applies as much to today's needs as it did ages ago.

Written to assist people in understanding and coping with change, the *I Ching* is a guide to *right conduct,* giving instruction about how to lead a successful and fulfilling life from birth until death. The *I Ching* describes the universe as a constantly moving and changing entity and tells how the *superior man* would behave under various challenging circumstances. In approximately 1200 B.C., King Wen, the Duke of Chou, and later Confucius expanded the earlier version of the *I Ching* that had originated with Fu Hsi. The book evolved over time becoming a written body of knowledge that further affected the practice of feng shui by giving it a formal structure.

From the 17th to the 20th centuries, Confucianism and Taoism (explained in Chapter 3) were joint state religions, and during this time the respect for beauty found in nature and the strict social order were

---

[6] Ibid, p. 11.

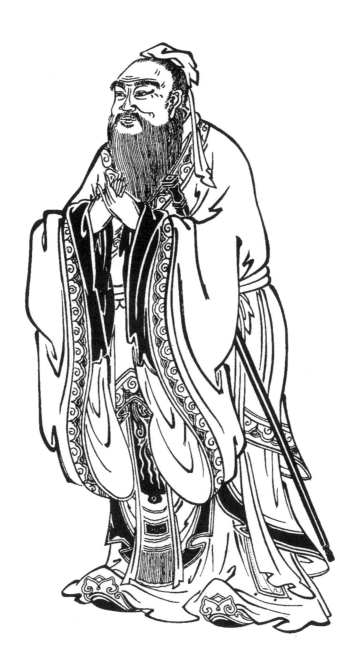

Confucius

at their heights. Education was highly prized, and only serious scholars could rise to an elevated status within the imperial court, which had extremely strict and formal criteria.

During this same period, an emphasis on the more delicate arts of painting, poetry, and calligraphy were required for the truly educated person. Chinese architecture came into its own, and perfection in landscaping became a highly specialized and prized skill. Over the centuries, this feng shui art of placement grew from a series of guidelines dealing with resting-places for the dead, into an active philosophy of designing homes for the living.

2

Feng Shui Wisdom

"The most powerful thing is an idea whose time has come."
— *Les Miserables*, Victor Hugo

Grace and Don had looked for a new home for several months. Their agent took them to a property just listed in an area where they hoped to relocate. When they approached the house at the very end of a cul-de-sac, they noticed a neighbor on the left dismantling his car engine in the driveway. The run-down home on the right had a trailer parked in front. Grace looked at Don with a raised eyebrow, and their agent commented, "This one might be a fixer-upper."

As Grace walked up the path, a thorny plant scratched her leg. Near the front door was a pile of old newspapers. The entry was small and dark, and they needed to walk around a large sofa to get into the living room. Since the owners had pulled most of the window shades down, their agent turned on several lights. They smelled a vague pet odor and stacks of old magazines were in several corners of the crowded dining room. Paperwork of some kind filled the kitchen table, and they found dishes in the sink and dirty pans on the stove.

By the time Grace and Don got to the bedrooms, they were not surprised to find the beds unmade and clothes on the floor. Having seen enough, they asked their agent to take them to the next house. Although this one might be a good buy and priced under market value, they wanted to say "goodbye."

Chi, the *Force* behind Feng Shui

Grace and Don were reacting to the *depressed energy* or what the Chinese call *stuck chi* — the poor energetic quality of the house that drove them out. Feng shui is based on the concept of chi, the unseen and powerful life-force that moves and flows throughout the universe. Sellers need to understand the concept of chi in order to fully comprehend and implement feng shui principles to help them sell their houses.

Literally translated as *life force* or *vitality,* according to feng shui, this *breath of life* permeates the cosmos: the earth, the land, nature, and ourselves. Chi makes up all persons, places, and things. Most cultures have this same concept of universal life energy. In Japan, it is called *ki*; in India, *prahna*; and for the ancient Romans, *spiritus* — the breath of life. It is called *pneuma* in Greek, r*uah* in Hebrew, and *rhor* in the Arabic language. Chi represents our *breath of nature,* our personal essence, and our spirit. Genesis 2:7 refers to essentially the same idea: "The Lord God formed man out of the clay of the ground and blew into his nostrils the breath of life, and so man became a living being."

Going with the Flow of Chi

Jami Lin, in her book *The Essence of Feng Shui*, applies this idea of chi to land formations and earth landscapes, and describes this energy that also exists within the earth. She explains, "...chi follows our planet's magnetic lines in circular, curvilinear patterns. It moves through the innermost parts of the globe and swells up in undulating currents as it nears the surface. There, it nurtures the land and all that dwells on it: plants, animals, and people."[7] Lush rain forests with clear streams, gentle topography, and abundant animal life contain a rich and strong flow of chi. The desert, with little water or vegetation of any kind and few animals contains weak and diminished chi. The comfort zone for most people lies somewhere in between these two extremes. We relax, and our inner spirit feels at peace when the environment surrounding us has healthy, abundant, and serene chi.

Stephen Skinner, in his excellent work *The Living Earth Manual of Feng Shui,* describes chi as "...being the life-blood of the living earth, and indirectly of the creatures... on its body, (it) fluctuates in much the same way as the pulses of the human body. Traditional Chinese medicine has always been much concerned with the measurements of various pulses at different points in the anatomy, drawing deductions about the state of health from the differences between each pulse rate. It is a natural extension, therefore, to expect that the health of the earth can be determined by checking the pulse or cyclical phase of the chi. As chi (of the earth) concentrates and disperses, or grows, flourishes and decays, a feng shui practitioner

---

[7] *The Essence of Feng Shui*, Jami Lin, p. 9.

needs to know at any point in space or time the cyclical phase of the chi." [8]

Ambiance Raised to a Higher Level

Feng shui teaches that chi gives each individual his or her personal drive or zest for life. When we have energy, health, and happiness, our chi goes up, and we feel powerful and invigorated, as if we can do almost anything. When we suffer from illness or depression, or when we experience grief and sadness, our chi goes down or gets stuck. We lack enthusiasm, and we feel weak and vulnerable. When we die, the soul, our life force, our chi, leaves the body.

Chi affects our attitude and reflects our health; similarly, the chi that exists within our homes moves freely or feels blocked. Since our homes are mirrors of our personalities, chi affects our dwellings in a similar way. We speak of the atmosphere or ambiance within a home or a room, much like we speak of our mood or attitude. "This place feels comfortable. This is a happy house. I like it here. This home feels good."

The River of Chi

To understand how chi works, think of water moving through a riverbed. When water rushes in straight lines or narrow pathways, it moves quickly, forcefully, and it can damage the riverbanks by its

---

[8] *The Living Earth Manual*, Stephen Skinner, p. 116.

22

continuing, relentless, and powerful energy. When water gently meanders in a river or stream, its power slows down, and the energy disperses and becomes more gentle. The water does no damage, and the curving riverbed channels the water, moving it from point to point, evenly distributing the force of the water, making the energy of the river more peaceful. We will apply this principle later in this book to front pathways to the porch and long interior hallways.

Visualize again what happens when the water in a river or stream does not circulate easily. It pools in eddies, and it becomes blocked and cannot move on its own. The flow gets sluggish, debris gathers, and the water eventually becomes stagnant. When our homes have excess clutter, piles of debris and old newspapers, heaps of laundry, and poorly positioned furnishings, chi cannot circulate freely and the energy gets blocked and cannot easily move through the space. This impedes the progress of chi, obstructs our energy and progress through the space, and makes inhabitants and guests feel uncomfortable.

This peaceful and tranquil chi moving throughout a space forms the basis of good feng shui. When houses have this gentle, welcoming, and comfortable quality, they appeal to us and make us feel at home. *A buyer wants to settle in and experience this tranquility in his or her own life.* Often the buyer will not realize that they are beginning to bond with the home that has good chi.

Buyers experience this sensitivity on an energetic or subconscious level. When this happens, an experienced agent notices that buyers slow down, taking their time as they enjoy each room. Prospective purchasers are savoring the home like a fine meal. They do not want to be rushed or hurried along at this point. This is *not* when the broker needs to start talking about the property's many amenities — the buyer is already picking up on those. It is much wiser for the agent to be quiet. The buyer is processing the home through all the filters they feel necessary. To do this well, they do not need any help, and talk only becomes a distraction at this point. The home either sells itself, or it does not.

When Buyers' Eyes Are Smiling

Often, when finding the home they both love, a couple will not have to say anything to each other, they simply walk through the house smiling. A comfort zone of internal delight is operating at this point, and good feng shui is at work. Buyers now begin to imagine their own possessions inside *your* space. They go through a definite process of thinking how to place their furniture and where each favorite piece will fit.

The wise real estate agent will encourage the buyers to take their time. To rush this process will break the spell. The longer it takes the buyer to proceed through this intellectual and emotional exercise, the better. This is an important decision. *They are mentally moving in.* On a practical level, when a buyer has reached this point and if your price makes sense to them, you can *usually* expect to receive an offer to purchase.

The Overwhelming House

Homebuyers Betty and Chuck came back to see two particular homes for the second time. Chuck's work was transferring him, and they needed to make a decision as soon as possible. They found things they liked about each of the properties and felt that today they would make a final choice.

The first house had a great floor plan and a potentially nice yard, but Betty had a hard time imagining their furniture in this home. The color scheme contained various shades of brick red, and throughout each room, red dominated the color scheme. The lady of the house avidly collected plants and had potted flowers of every sort on each windowsill and in every corner. Plants hung from the ceiling and several sat on each table. Outside, the landscaping was overgrown with shrubbery. Both Betty and Chuck walked through the house and around the property several times, but they felt overwhelmed by the plants and the forceful color on so many walls. They could not really see the home, let alone focus on how their own furnishings would fit.

In the second house, they realized that the floor plan was not quite as functional as the first one, and it actually had less square footage. However, in this house the owners had a more neutral color scheme and very few furnishings. The flow of the house felt pleasant and workable; Betty told Chuck she thought their furniture would fit just fine. Although the rooms were slightly smaller, they thought this house would work for them. Their agent told them they could easily paint the first house and have the benefit of the larger home; but both Chuck and Betty decided, after

talking it over, the smaller house just felt better to them, and they
thought they would be quite comfortable there.

It's All in the Balance of Yin and Yang

The second essential concept of bringing good feng shui into your home is balancing the qualities of yin and yang — two primordial and complementary forces that operate throughout the universe. This ancient concept reflects the fundamentals of Taoism (pronounced Daoism), which puts emphasis on the loveliness and perfection found in nature. Taoism views the unaffected yet rich brilliance of the natural world as the ultimate example of exquisite beauty. Our challenge, on a practical level, is to apply balanced aspects of yin and yang to our rigid, man-made world of houses, streets, towns, and cities.

Feng shui teaches that the ultimate balancing of the yin and yang elements of design and color within a space benefit the flow of auspicious chi and eventually lead to a serene, comfortable, and welcoming home. In the story of Betty and Chuck, the first house was predominantly yang with too much plant life and strong color. An appropriate number of healthy plants is great, but this was simply too much of a good thing. A jungle belongs in a rainforest, not in the interior of a house.

Further, people cannot adjust to the shade of red, in large doses, as it contains the most yang of all colors and carries too much power and aggressive energy. In a living space, a little red used as an accent or one wall in a shade of red, works great for zest, but most comfortable houses want to have the quality of a gentle villa, not the Moulin Rouge!

As Professor Lin Yun and Sarah Rossbach describe in their book, ***Living Color***, "Yin is dark, while yang is light. Yin is female; yang is male. Yin is passive; yang is active. Together, yin and yang create a harmonious whole — the Tao. They are interdependent: without cold, the concept of heat does not exist; without an outside, there is no inside; without life, there is no death. These opposites exist within each other: within the male, there is a bit of the female, and vice versa. Through the complementary opposites of yin and yang, the Chinese link man to heaven and earth." [9] The yin/yang symbol depicts a small dot of the white within the larger black shape, and a tiny spot of the black within the larger white. Taoism teaches that in order to achieve and maintain true balance, it is necessary for some of the opposing essence to be found within the other. The dot represents that without one, the other cannot exist. [10]

Feng shui encourages the use of authentic examples from nature in our living space and fewer man-made or synthetic materials whenever possible. Natural fabrics such as cotton, ramie, linen, and authentic textures of wood, stone, or slate are suggested whenever possible. Try placing skylights in dark areas instead of using artificial light. The feng shui rule of thumb is to think natural. In applying this principle to our living spaces, the closer we get to the inner and outer balance we seek, the more this gently powerful technique counters the overwhelming stress and anxiety of our frenzied, modern lives. As our

---

[9] *Living Color*, Master Lin Yun and Sarah Rossbach, p. 21.
[10] Ibid.

dwellings become more orderly, tranquil, and esthetically natural, we gain inner harmony and feel more in tune with the natural order.

To help readers understand how to design the kind of natural living space that would work wonders for the seller, and appeal to buyers, Laurel Lund, the former Editor in Chief of *Natural Home Magazine,* describes this concept as "… creating a healthy, harmonious home environment in which you and your family can thrive… surrounding yourself not only with the people and things you love, but also with furnishings and finishes that are natural and non-toxic… constructing dwellings with sustainable, renewable resources that don't deplete the earth's own precious supply… choosing décor that nurtures body and soul… clean air and fresh water, paint that doesn't pollute… creating a sanctuary where you can be the best you can be — in short, a place to come home to. It means living with vitality, at one with nature, at one with yourself." [11]

To cultivate this natural type of lifestyle, balance colors, textures, shapes, and design elements within a living space. Compared to the concept of chi, the balancing of yin and yang qualities requires subtlety. Listed below, the Table of Opposites illustrates the application of yin and yang in nature.

---

[11] *Natural Home Magazine*™, May-June 1999, p. 8.

Yang	Yin
Heaven	Earth
Sun	Moon
Male	Female
Hot	Cool
Dry	Moist
Light	Dark
Large	Small
High	Low
Hard	Soft
Sharp	Dull
Straight	Curved
Angular	Round
Geometric	Floral
Loud	Quiet

When using yin and yang design applications within your home to achieve a serene and harmonious setting, remember that *rounded* edges of picture frames and mirrors will help to balance lots of pointed corners and 90 degree angles within a room, shawls or afghans draped over pointy corners will soften angular furniture such as chairs and sofas, and rounded corners on dining room and coffee tables will produce a more energetically gentle quality within a room than furniture with hard or pointed ones. The Taoist influence in feng shui teaches that beauty and tranquility is all in the *balance* of these two design extremes.

The Magic of the Five Elements

After understanding the concepts of chi and yin and yang, the next fundamental idea to grasp is that of the *Five Elements*. According to feng shui, everything in the natural world can be classified into the elements Earth, Metal, Water, Wood, and Fire. Since our dwellings are microcosms of our larger planetary home we can apply this thinking to all the colors, textures, shapes, and design elements within our houses.

Each of the five elements contains both a gentle (yin) and a powerful (yang) force or aspect to their energy. For example, imagine a powerful, crashing surf pounding the shoreline. This intensity can demolish piers, destroy buildings, and gouge rocky cliffs — this energy of the Water element is yang. Now imagine a deep, placid lake surrounded by perfect calm with a mirror-like surface. You hear no sound except gentle ripples at its edge. In this case the element of Water is very yin.

To further illustrate, even if red were your favorite color it would not be a balanced application to paint an entire room, especially one intended as a bedroom, bright red. Red represents the element of Fire and the most yang of all the colors. Most people are not comfortable for too long in spaces that are too energetically yang. Yang colors work great in restaurants or recreational centers where the function and purpose of the space is meant to be lively and filled with upbeat or intense energy. However, in homes intended for serene living, an excess of yang design elements usually isn't appropriate. Touches of red in various shades work wonderfully as accents and to provide a point of interest, but in order to balance a room with tranquility in mind, an excess of yang energy is out of equilibrium, and the space will just not *feel* right to most people.

As stated earlier, feng shui deals with how a house feels and aims to balance the yin and yang of both the natural and man-made aspects within our homes. Experienced interior designers and most artists do this intuitively, as if they have a built-in sense of natural feng shui. They might not understand *why* they arrange furnishings and design pieces beautifully within a space; they do it because they know it *feels better* that way — this is a demonstration of *intuitive* feng shui. Learning this is not difficult, and you too can do it with a little understanding and practice.

The Language of the Elements, one of the most powerful feng shui applications for interior decorating, balances and enhances the chi within a space. The Five Elements make up the building blocks of feng shui, and when used within each area or room, further create a feeling of design and energetic equilibrium. Specific shapes, colors, seasons, and compass directions represent each element. As illustrated in the following chart, the pointed, triangular shape similar to a flame, the color red, the season of summer, and the South, symbolizes the Element of Fire. Earth correlates to the square or rectangle, the color yellow (or earth tones), mid-autumn, and Southwest. The circle, white or silver (also jewel-tones), autumn, and West symbolizes Metal. The Water Element correlates to an amorphous fluid shape, dark blue or black, winter, and North. A cylindrical or trunk-like shape, green for all growing plant life, the season of spring, and East all represent the Element of Wood.

The Five Elements affect each other according to their particular sequence or order. Two distinct cycles exist and have specific feng shui design applications. In the Nurturing (or Generating) cycle, the Elements feed, or amplify, each other in succession: Fire produces ash (Earth), Earth contains Metal (ore), Metal holds Water (as in a bowl), Water nourishes Wood, and Wood feeds Fire. In the Controlling cycle, the Elements counter-balance each other: Metal chops Wood, Wood displaces Earth (as roots delve into soil), Earth dams Water, Water extinguishes Fire, and Fire melts Metal.

When balancing elements within a room, the feng shui goal is to have all the elements represented. If one element dominates, such as in a living room with white walls, a white sofa, a metal coffee table, metal frames around paintings, and plants in brass pots, the Element of Metal is very emphasized. To control this heavy metal room, the controlling Element of Fire can be brought in, such as in a burgundy area rug under the coffee table and red tapestry throw pillows on the sofa. Additional plants will introduce the Wood Element and a simple table-top fountain would bring in Water.

THE FIVE ELEMENTS MAP
Nourishing and Controlling Relationships

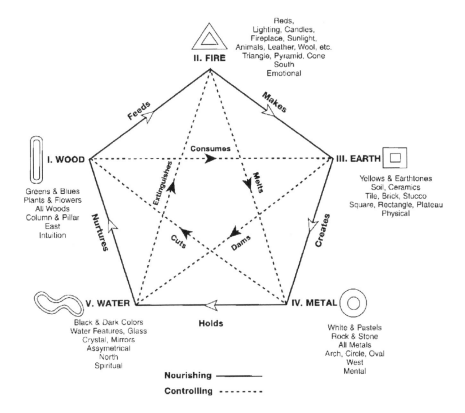

The Nurturing and Controlling Cycles of the Five Elements
(Graphic courtesy of Terah Kathryn Collins and Hay House Publishing Co.)

Feng shui uses these two cycles to ensure that a room is balanced elementally. If all of the Five Elements exist within a space and that space does not contain too much of any one particular element, it produces a feeling of comfort and internal harmony. If, however, you have a room out of balance, perhaps with too much Metal, using some of its controlling element of Fire will help create balance.

For example, imagine a room painted white, with light off-white carpet, metal picture frames on the walls, a bronze sculpture in one corner, and in front of the white sofa, a circular glass coffee table with metal legs. This room is overly weighted toward the Metal element. To bring it back into feng shui alignment, add touches of the controlling Fire Element such as a deep burgundy area rug under the coffee table, a still life painting on the wall of red-hued flowers, or some deep red candles on the coffee table. Use the other elements of Water, Wood, and Earth in the room to feel in feng shui balance. Don't use much Earth, since Earth creates Metal in the nurturing cycle.

Now you have the basic concepts of chi, yin and yang, and the Five Elements. As you become more familiar with using these feng shui tools, you will find yourself placing furnishings and using color and shape within your home to your best advantage. As I teach my feng shui classes, these fundamental ideas need to be understood before proceeding further in applying feng shui principles to room arrangement and interior design. In order to use this ancient design science and practice it on a level that will help sell your house, try to incorporate these concepts into your decorating whenever possible to achieve a harmonious and balanced quality within each room.

Location, Location, Location

Feng shui takes this familiar phrase of the real estate world back about 4,000 years to the days when the ancient Chinese built the Imperial City and the Temple of Heaven in Beijing, designed the Ming Tombs, and constructed the White Pyramid of The Empress Wu. In the formalized, traditional feng shui of old, they laid out these famous sites on a north-south axis and carefully evaluated the ideal feng shui position to achieve a site having both support and harmony. The most auspicious site had a hill behind the structure with protective stands of trees, foliage or gentle land formations to the right and left, and a lower hill in front, preferably with an element of water such as a pond or a stream in the extreme foreground.

On a symbolic level, these celestial animals were chosen to represent the four sacred directions and other natural elements. The green dragon on the east symbolizes spring, the element of wood, and the rising sun. To the west, the white tiger stands for the element of metal, and the season of autumn and harvest. In the south, the red phoenix bird represents the element of fire and summer. Completing the cycle, in the north, the black tortoise indicates the element of water and winter. Man, anchored in the soil or earth, represents the fifth element at the center of this cosmic map. [12] Where the green dragon and white tiger joined in an embrace in the classic feng shui armchair position would be the ideal building site.

---

[12] *The Chinese House*, Ronald G. Knapp, p. 56.

Classic Feng Shui Armchair Position for Site Placement

Today some of the most expensive real estate not only in the West, but also worldwide, often sits a bit higher up on a hill than lower priced homes. It probably has some privacy, protective elements around it such as tall trees or foliage on either side, and an ocean or other panoramic view out to the front. Many buyers would choose this site if they could afford the best.

An excellent location in real estate contains more than just a good view on a nice parcel of land. The ideal property also contains a number of quality essentials: privacy, view, gentle terrain, realistic proximity to necessary services, and a well-designed dwelling suitable to the buyer's needs. Beauty is always in the eye of the beholder, and each buyer has his or her own criteria as to what will evoke a smile and a decision to write an offer to purchase.

Example of a Home in the Feng Shui Armchair Position

Of course, the location you have as a seller is not going to change, and you must work with the site you have. ***In order to not lose a single prospect, you want to make your home and property stand out as an excellent buy among all the other houses in your neighborhood that are in a similar price range.*** Now, as you begin to view real estate with new feng shui eyes, you will see how easily you can use this design science to help prepare your home to sell.

3

The Schools of Feng Shui

"In choosing your dwelling, know how to keep to the ground. In cultivating your mind, know how to dive into the hidden depths. In making a move, know how to choose the right moment."

— Lao Tsu

A college history professor, Brad, had been trying to sell his condominium for several months. He and his girlfriend Amy had decided to marry and buy a larger home together. His listing agent and other brokers had brought a number of potential buyers to preview his home, but there have been no takers. Wanting to speed up the selling process and trying not to be discouraged, he followed Amy's advice to learn about the ancient Chinese design philosophy called feng shui. Amy was convinced it would help him sell his condo.

To Brad's surprise, his favorite bookstore had over 40 books on the subject. They covered topics such as feng shui in the home, the garden, the office, the apartment, the bedroom, and the workplace. Some of the books were the coffee table type; some were how-to manuals, and others were quite specific regarding subjects such as improving one's romantic life, increasing abundance, enhancing fame, and embarking on a new career. Puzzled as to where to start, Brad looked over several rather generic looking texts to decide which book would give him the best basic advice.

He found one that talked about the direction in which he slept, cooked his food, ate his meals, and sat at his desk. In that book, the compass illustration showed North positioned at the bottom where South normally is. He wondered how he would deal with that. As his confusion grew, Brad knew that he wanted just the essential feng shui philosophy for selling his condo, so he decided to focus on one that seemed more fundamental.

Another book spoke about how to place furnishings, how to create a feeling of harmony and serenity within a space, and how to balance the design elements in a home. This book talked a lot about clearing the interior space first in order for feng shui to work well. It paid special attention to setting a firm intention regarding whatever it was the occupant wanted to create within their life, and gave guidelines for solutions on how to achieve these goals.

Brad realized that his home, despite its good location, was filled with too much stuff that would turn off potential buyers. He knew he needed to work on clearing all this clutter right away. Now his intention was to get this place sold! Which approach to feng shui should he follow?

Doing Your Home Work — the Schools of Feng Shui

You will grasp the feng shui homework you need to sell your home more easily if you understand the various points of view of this design science. Learning the secrets and techniques of feng shui is like putting on a new set of glasses. They help you view your home, furnishings, yard, entire parcel of land, and even your garage in a new and refreshing way. As with many other fields of study (including architecture, medicine, and chiropractic) there are different schools of thought or philosophies. Each viewpoint teaches a slightly different method for achieving the desired results.

This chapter helps the beginning feng shui student understand these different approaches. Learning to identify and distinguish among them will assist you in selecting additional books for further reading and applying feng shui principles to your home. *Note that within each school the fundamental concept of achieving harmony and balance within a space is constant.* Whether you eventually follow Compass, Black Tibetan Sect, or any other feng shui viewpoint, the delightful rewards and underlying reasons for re-creating space remain the same.

The Form School — Under All is the Land

Feng shui began over 3,000 years ago in the south of China with what is called the Form or Land Form School. In this region of China, the immense and rugged mountain peaks, typical of the Guilin area, descend into tranquil lakes and rivers. When in Guilin, one almost feels they are in an extra-terrestrial world. I have visited these spectacular land formations, and the scenery is beautiful almost beyond description.

Unique Land Formations in the Guilin Region of Southwest China

In ancient times, the chi or life force associated with the landscape took on highly symbolic meaning, and this idea continues to the present. Today *the back of the dragon* still refers to mountain ridge tops, prominent outcroppings and rock formations which hold special energy considered too yang for human comfort. One is always encouraged not to place a home or temple, or to dig foundations into the earth in these areas and thus disturb the sleeping dragon!

Man's relationship with these natural land formations took on important significance for feng shui and its origins in the Form School. The mythical symbolism the early Chinese saw in certain geographic formations affected their decisions regarding where to site graves, plant crops, place temples, palaces, and later homes. These judgments took advantage of the best chi, or *breath of life*, that nature had to offer, yielding abundant harvests and fostering orderly development within growing towns and villages.

Out of intuitive wisdom, the early feng shui masters developed this science by observing natural phenomena including the shapes of mountains, where the water flowed, where the soil was sweetest, and where the sun gave its greatest warmth. Early feng shui was simple common sense, and learned scholars were quick to point out that the auspicious placement of structures along feng shui guidelines had beneficial and wondrous results. They felt that adherence to these concepts brought harmony and fortunate blessings into the lives of the inhabitants while providing security and greater abundance for the community.

As explained in Chapter 2, the best feng shui location has an aspect of strength and protection in the rear, a small rise or mound in the front and ideally a view of water in the front. Lush foliage or natural terrain shapes on either side provided privacy and a sense of having a haven-like shelter from the outside world. Ideally, the dragon formation on the left of the dwelling would be at least slightly higher than the tiger element on the right, since it is felt the dragon must always keep the tiger under control. The best position for building is where the dragon and tiger join in symbolic embrace. This ideal site is the focus of good feng shui.

It is understood, however, that few sites in the normal landscape are perfect. This is where feng shui practitioners would be called in to diagnose the location, to make recommendations for improving the chi, and to diminish any negative elements. The ancient Chinese understood chi as moving along these earth dragon-lines (areas of especially powerful energy) in a way that is similar to how acupuncture works with the flow of energy along the meridian lines in the human body.

The ancient Chinese looked at nature as a living, breathing organism, and they revered its powers and the mysteries of the invisible world. The influence of Taoism brought a belief that living in harmony with nature was the essence of environmental and topographical perfection. They strongly perceived that combining this philosophy of natural beauty with feng shui led to good fortune, encouraged auspicious opportunities in one's life, caused a feeling of harmony within the spirit, and brought abundance into the household.

Whenever possible, people were encouraged to enhance their inside space with the loveliness found outside in the natural world. Windows were placed to frame a beautiful view; lush trees, vibrant foliage, subtle shades of blooming flowers, and meandering streams were all considered ideal vistas on which to focus.

When building homes and designing landscapes, nature would be re-created and copied using water fountains, sheltered arbors, and verdant gardens. Shapes would be gentle and rounded, since natural elements seldom have rigid corners and harsh edges. The moon gate found in Asian landscape and garden design is especially beautiful with its striking rounded portal; it provides the ideal, almost magical, transition between one space and another — earth and heaven, the masculine yang and the feminine yin, the inner dwelling and the outside world.

Moongate in Shanghai Garden

Form School principles permeate current feng shui practice and both of the other schools. Because its primary principles acknowledge and honor the importance of land and its shapes and contours, every major current application also uses this precept to some degree. Therefore, understanding the Form School is understanding basic feng shui.

Quoting Feng Shui Master, Professor Wong, "...(Feng shui is) probably the earliest form of environmental protectionism; it taught that to destroy or pollute the earth is to destroy man's natural base. To improve one's self and to enjoy the environment is fundamental. The key element is selecting a site — the design of the house is secondary. A building should become a part of the site, and luxury does not necessarily equal good feng shui." [13]

The Compass School

In the north of China, where the topography is less mountainous and relatively flat in comparison to the more striking geography to the south and west, a second school of feng shui developed in the latter part of 900 C.E. known as the Compass School. Sometimes called the Hokkien School, this very traditional approach determines the most auspicious site for a dwelling by using a specially designed feng shui compass called a *luo pan*.

This ancient handheld device has a small glass-covered circular opening in the center, and within this Heaven Pool, a magnetic needle

---

[13] Feng shui intensive class taught by Master Prof. Wong in Beijing. China. Feng Shui Immersion Study Tour with Helen and James Jay, Oct. 2000.

points south. Because Compass School relies on direction for its application of feng shui solutions, the luo pan method calculates the most auspicious compass alignment that the site or house faces according to the occupant's birth charts, which are based on the Chinese lunar calendar and when the house was constructed. In addition, because south is the direction of warmth and where the gentle and benevolent winds arise, it is very favorable feng shui for a home to face south.

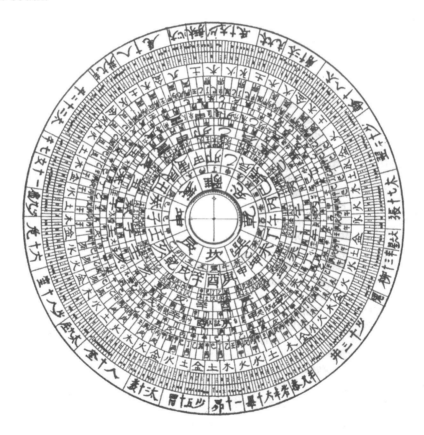

Antique Luo-Pan Used by Early Feng Shui Masters

In the Compass School, before using any of the cures to adjust poorly moving chi, the luo pan determines the exact north-south axis of the dwelling. Because of its primary importance, south is always found at the top of the feng shui compass. It is felt there is an advantage to this positioning since this is the direction you would look out your front door if you were in a house with an ideal south-facing location. [14] The difficulty for some Westerners with using this approach lies partly in the positioning of north at the bottom of the compass when determining direction; east is found on the left and west on the right.

After determining the precise direction of the dwelling, the Compass School practitioner uses the pa kua (refer to Appendix A), an octagonal energy template, and applies it to the home's floor plan to locate the most auspicious and least favorable directions for a person's home or office. The pa kua shows the *I Ching* trigrams associated with the eight feng shui Life Sectors and how they align with the compass directions. In Compass School teaching, the Fame sector of the trigrams is always aligned to magnetic South with the remaining seven sectors falling into place accordingly. Going deeper and following ancient Chinese tradition, the numerology associated with the magic square, or lo shu, is yet another determining factor for a person's best directions.

Compass School has a very large following in many countries, especially the United States, Great Britain, and Germany. It suits all levels of students, especially those followers of feng shui who wish to focus on a traditional, classical, and somewhat analytic approach.

---

[14] Ibid.

Black Sect Tantric Buddhism Feng Shui
(BTB or Black Hat)

A more recent school of feng shui, Black Sect Tantric Buddhism (BTB), blends Tibetan Tantric Buddhism, Taoism, the wisdom of the *I Ching*, and spiritual mysticism. Grand Master Professor Thomas Lin Yun brought BTB feng shui to the West from China several decades ago. This approach designates the main entrance to the home or office as the all-important *mouth of chi*. The architect and builder set up this alignment of front door energy when the home is originally designed and constructed. The primary door that the contractor intends is the official mouth of chi, even if occupants use another entrance more frequently.

The BTB School also uses the mystical eight-sided figure of the bagua. *The pa kua of the Compass method and the bagua of BTB are synonymous,* each side representing a different aspect of life. The bagua, with the trigrams of the *I Ching,* is at the core of feng shui and is used as the energy template for sites, dwellings, and offices. The bagua has many layers of application and can be placed over the floor plan of a home, the surface of a desktop, a windowsill, or a corporate building. In BTB feng shui, all other aspects of the bagua's eight Life Sectors align in the dwelling to determine the location (not the direction) of the front door.

In BTB feng shui, the bagua template is considered to be energetically within the individual as well as inside the physical space of the home. It is as if the compass is *internalized.* We become the compass in a sense.[15] This school presents a somewhat more functional

---

[15] Feng shui lecture with Helen and James Jay, Nanjing, China. Oct., 2000.

method of implementing feng shui cures or solutions for a wide variety of inherent design problems. The chi of the dwelling is assessed for smooth and easy flow, and specific feng shui remedies are recommended wherever a particular sector of the home needs a particular chi adjustment.

BTB feng shui goes beyond the placement of cures or feng shui solutions and emphasizes the importance of setting one's intention regarding what changes the occupants wish to bring about in their lives. Positive results are credited to the dedication and sincerity of the one who speaks these intentions and sets the goal as the feng shui solution to adjust the chi is put in place. BTB feng shui teachings have a very large following, especially in the United States.

Intuitive Feng Shui

Occasionally one hears a reference made to intuitive feng shui. This refers more to an innate sense of beauty and design smarts found among many artists, interior designers, architects, and other creative people. Like a sixth sense, many people have a built-in knowing about how to harmoniously place things, how to decorate for a feeling of balance, and how to select design appointments that feed the spirit as well as the five senses.

Intuitive feng shui is not a true school, however, and should be thought of more as an inherent talent or skill. We have all visited homes where we immediately feel at ease and thoroughly enjoy being in that particular place — we want to stay. Whoever decorated and put that space together probably possesses a good sense of intuitive feng shui.

However, traditional feng shui uses a clear set of guidelines and solutions to correct design difficulties and to unblock chi. This age-old environmental structure provides the grammar for this language of intentional and serene living. If a practitioner only applies intuitive feng shui, they miss the underlying concepts or rules, the *grammar* if you will, of this perceptive and specific design science.

Even though feng shui is deliberate in its methods, it encourages intuition. No matter which school of feng shui you follow, the end result of the interior design should feel good on an intuitive as well as a practical level. However, you are encouraged to venture beyond the intuitive practitioners and seek out feng shui consultants who will give you fundamental and bona fide reasons for whatever adjustments are to be made.

Eliminate the Negative Sha Arrows

All the various schools of feng shui teach about *sha* chi or *killing breath.* These are the negative arrows of cutting, man-made or natural energy. When pointed at a dwelling, these poison arrows are believed to bring misfortune or disaster into one's life. They create energetic discomfort and have a subtle threatening aspect. Sha chi can take the form of forceful wind, sharp corners of nearby buildings, acute roof lines of neighboring houses, electric power lines, telephone poles, satellite dishes, even business signs. Sha chi is any element that seems to dominate, protrude, or aim toward a building in a negative or energetically harmful way.

Feng shui also discourages the placement of dwellings on mountaintops or hilltops where there is no shelter from the cutting and forceful sha winds. The view might be great, but to build in such a place invites physical discomfort and reduces the occupants' ability to go outside and enjoy the beauty of nature. They end up staying indoors to avoid being buffeted by the very yang *feng* or constant wind energy. When visiting China, one observes that temples, pagodas, and homes are all built slightly down the hillside, usually about one-third of the way from the top. This siting allows for lovely views yet also provides protection to the rear of the structure and removes the building from the winds at the summit.

Inside a home, negative arrows take the form of sharp corners from interior walls, cornered tables, other furniture, or any pointy design element. Heavy or dark colored large beams over beds or dining room tables are discouraged since they carry oppressive or heavy chi. This sha energy comes in the form of any element carrying negative associations. Eliminate, deflect, or neutralize these unpleasant energetic forces by means of a feng shui cure, such as a mirrored surface, a wind chime, a faceted crystal positioned inside, or bagua mirror placed outside, usually above the front door.

Mirrors, often referred to as the aspirin of feng shui, are frequently used for a variety of design challenges. The rule for mirrors is usually the larger the better. Hang mirrors slightly higher than the tallest person in the home, so that person does not have to stoop to see their facial image or feel energetically cut off. Mirror tiles are usually not recommended because they break up and distort the reflected chi.

The use of mirrors can push energy away or pull energy forward. Mirrors also act to double the abundance, as on a stove, tabletop, or near a cash register. It is often recommended that they not be placed opposite a front door in an entryway because a mirror will reflect back the benevolent and welcoming chi that you want to encourage to circulate within. (Putting a mirror on a side wall would be a better choice.)

Positioned above our desks on the wall, mirrors show who walks behind us if our back is to the doorway. They also energetically and visually camouflage surfaces that protrude or are unsightly for any reason. An excellent example of interior application of mirrors on square pillars inside a commercial space can be seen at the Airport Restaurant in Monterey, California. Within this relatively small dining area, mirror panels completely cover each side of the square interior pillars and have the effect of making them beautifully disappear.

Feng shui viewpoints differ on the use of mirrors in the bedroom. Since mirrors multiply what they reflect, they are a strong yang element. Bedrooms are yin rooms since their function is for rest and repose. To have exceptionally large mirrors in bedrooms, such as on closet doors, may energetically disturb the occupant's sleep, especially if the mirrors directly reflect the bed. However, if the room is dark and needs the enhancement of available light, mirrors will help. Here is where intuition, sensitivity, and design sense come into play. If the occupant sleeps just fine, leaving the mirrored doors probably will not create a feng shui problem. Another solution would be to drape them with attractive fabric during the night while sleeping.

Choosing a Feng Shui Book Today

Ten years ago, very few books regarding feng shui were available; today things are quite different. Approach the home arts section of most bookstores, and you will see an amazing array of feng shui volumes from which to choose, each one written from the perspective of the author's particular school. When shopping, keep in mind that feng shui can be learned on many levels. If you are a beginner, then start with a simple and fundamental text.

If a novice selects an intermediate or advanced book, they can easily become bewildered. Some readers who inadvertently plunge into the deeper (or higher) levels of feng shui from the start get frustrated and want to fling the whole idea out the window! Visit the library or bookstores and look through various books. If the author frequently mentions the north, south, east, and west directions and frequently uses the spelling pa kua, you are most likely looking at a Compass School text. If the book frequently refers to the setting of intention, omits compass directions, and uses the spelling bagua, you are probably examining a Black Tibetan Sect volume.

Because most feng shui titles are tempting, remember that the overall goal of harmony and balance within a space is fundamental to all schools of feng shui; that does not change. However, some techniques and methods of obtaining results are particular to certain points of view. As you understand these differences, this information will help you clearly choose which method or school works best for you.

As I give feng shui guidance to my clients who are *selling* real estate, I usually teach them BTB because they are moving on, and their best direction will not serve them in this dwelling much longer. I do not want them to feel more anchored to this space, and their intention to sell is fundamental to the process. Quite the contrary, I am encouraging them to energetically let go and welcome the chi of the new buyer. The main idea is getting the chi of the house to move easily and gently, remove the clutter, and let the beauty of nature in wherever possible. When marketing a home, these BTB guidelines serve sellers well and bring fast results.

Working with *buyers* is a different feng shui matter altogether! They usually intend to stay in this new home for quite a while. In these cases, when the buyers pay attention to their best directions, a Compass School approach is extremely helpful and provides them with maximum feng shui wisdom. Next is the combination of this information with specific site data that includes what to look for on a parcel of land no matter how large or small and what to seek as well as what to avoid in a floor plan.

If you are selling, you are likely buying (or getting ready to buy) — watch for my next book, *Buy Your Home SMARTER with Feng Shui*. Detailed information on the important feng shui aspects of acquiring real estate as well as explicit professional tips will help buyers. Serious students of feng shui should also refer to the Bibliography for additional feng shui and real estate texts.

Back to the Future

Some houses sell quickly while others never seem to budge. When a buyer *experiences* a prospective home they have an emotional and inner response to it. Buyers either feel good as they walk through a house or they don't. No matter how much a property may be priced as a bargain, a purchaser will not buy if they do not connect with the home on an inner level — especially these days when prices are relatively high. For all the money they will spend, they are buying a *feeling* as well as paying for a roof and four walls.

Many adherents of feng shui believe that most of us will want to design our homes in the future using this design philosophy. Feng shui's resurgence feels real, and it seems that as long as the busy pace of daily life stays at its current rate, this eco-science of placement, harmony, and balance is here to stay. Considering the stress levels of our modern world, we seem guided from within to seek out new and different ways to achieve a sense of equilibrium in our lives. Feng shui is one of those ways.

Far from a trendy fad, this design technique shares its broad-based appeal with people from all occupations and lifestyles. Its widespread use cuts across economic and political lines. Not a religion but a philosophy, feng shui appeals to people of all faiths, ethnic groups, and levels of education. Its wisdom is attractive to mainstream thinking because we have come to realize that our species needs help to recoup a sense of ourselves in a quieter, gentler way. Whether we are looking for grounding or serenity in our lives to help find these qualities in our living space — whether we are buying or selling real estate, feng shui is here to serve us.

Section II

Tools for Change...

Use the Power of Feng Shui to Sell Your House

... from The Prophet

Then a mason came forth and said,

Speak to us of Houses.
And he (Almustafa, the chosen and the beloved)
answered and said:

...Your house is your larger body. It grows in the sun and
sleeps in the stillness of the night; and it is not dreamless.
Does not your house dream?
And dreaming, leave the city for grove or hill-top?

...Your house shall be not an anchor but a mast...
for that which is boundless in you
abides in the mansion of the sky,
whose door is the morning mist, and
whose windows are the songs and
the silences of night.

— Kahlil Gibran

4

Clear Your Clutter —
Feng Shui's Prime Directive

"Most of the luxuries, and many of the so-called comforts of life, are not only dispensable, but positive hindrances to the elevation of humanity."

— Henry David Thoreau

Lucille was in her mid-sixties and living in the big house where she and her husband had raised their family. Hal died several years ago and now her married children and their families lived in Seattle. Lucille wanted to sell her home and move closer to her children. Her friend who sold real estate had nicely, but firmly, told her that although her "things" were lovely, the house was so full a buyer wouldn't be able to concentrate on its finer qualities because of all the decorations, knick-knacks, and paintings.

How could she begin the task of removing objects filled with so many memories? Hal's hunting gear and ham radio equipment, along with rows and rows of her collector plates, and her cupboards filled with antique dolls all overwhelmed her. Her new home would be much smaller and easier to care for, but had no room for all this stuff. Lucille also realized she really did not want it all anymore; it was time to lighten up as she prepared to move away.

Lucille soon found that the local historical society accepted quality collections for donations to their new museum. She discovered that the neighborhood thrift store, which supported the developmentally disabled, would take any usable items. Two telephone calls was all it took to solve these problems.

Relieved, Lucille called her son and daughter who were delighted to hear she was thinking of relocating closer to them and that she had lightened her load of possessions. They did not need any thing from her, and they encouraged her to let go of those things she did not want to bring. Now she and her agent could put the house up for sale. Happily, Lucille was almost on her way.

Our Home is Like a Mirror

Feng shui philosophy helps us understand that our homes are a direct reflection of our inner selves, much like an environmental mirror. Our personal space tells the world what kind of people we are: creative, organized, distinctive, fancy, simple, serene, or something unique. As time passes, our lifestyles and needs change; possessions we thought essential, and possessions we treasured, we no longer need. Such a realization is difficult, but when it comes to selling our home, we need to concentrate on getting rid of everything that is not necessary, functional to the task at hand, or has ceased to bring us joy.

If you want a buyer to feel comfortable in your home, spend time there and concentrate on what your house has to offer, then the feng shui techniques presented in this book will give you the necessary guidance. This means that you, the seller, have to begin sorting through and removing unwanted possessions. Feng shui relies on order and simplicity. *Reduce* and *recycle* are the passwords to allow the good chi energy to flow. If you want to sell your home, and have it sell faster, begin to look around your house with feng shui eyes.

When the decision is made that you will soon be moving, this is the time to box up your extra possessions and store them elsewhere. As for the stuff you no longer need, have several garage sales. Or better yet, take them to a thrift store! In feng shui, when a space is crowded with too many things, the chi becomes blocked and is unable to circulate freely. In other words, there is no room for new opportunities and fortunate blessings to enter the home. A home that is too crowded and cluttered will not allow a potential buyer to move easily through the space and focus on all the good qualities of the house.

Clutter No Longer Serves You — or the Sale of Your House

Some time ago, I spent several years in the Persian Gulf teaching school in Saudi Arabia and Abu Dhabi; I became familiar with the Bedouin culture that still thrives in the vast deserts. These proud and self-sufficient nomadic people have a wonderfully simple motto when it comes to moving on to a new site, *"If it does not fit on the camel… it does not go to the next oasis."*

We can learn from the Bedouins and lighten up our own space, therefore, lightening up our lives. In our Western culture, we fill our houses, attics, basements, and garages with excess stuff. Then we pay more money to rent storage units (sometimes for years) to keep all of our precious belongings, many of which are in piles of unmarked boxes we have already forgotten about. We cart these things around; moving them from house to house, and then wonder why we feel so tired, confused, and distracted most of the time. Later in this book, I do recommend renting a storage unit *temporarily* during the process of selling your home. However, a storage rental is not a permanent solution to clutter!

Once the process of de-cluttering is complete, your home will be far more attractive and you will actually feel a mental and physical lift. Clutter and all the excess things with which we surround ourselves, represent blocked chi and will not help your house to sell!

Since this impeded energy weighs down upon the occupants and visitors, a potential buyer who enters a house with a distracting interior will feel bewildered, and find it difficult to concentrate. Bombarded by walls of family photographs and collectibles, coffee tables groaning with stacks of magazines, plants hanging from every corner, or piles of newspapers on the floor, can make a potential buyer feel distracted.

Collections that line your hallways or living room walls may be your pride and joy, but will tend to divert the buyer from paying close attention to the home itself. Later they may remember more about your antique photographs than the floor plan. A wise seller will put these items away and allow a purchaser to focus on the main features of the house.

On a typical house-hunting day, a buyer may visit five or six homes — anything more than that can be too much to absorb. Experienced agents know that previewing three homes is closer to the ideal. After three or four showings, buyers have to mentally sift through all the floor plans as well as weigh the advantages and disadvantages of each property. Details start to run together. You want your home to stand out as inviting and attractive, the one they want to return to. Agents are well aware buyers spend less time in a cluttered house. People naturally want to escape to a more serene and harmonious environment. Here is your chance to capture buyers' hearts; don't miss this opportunity!

When it comes to selling a home, clutter is usually your worst enemy. The more you eliminate, the faster your property will sell. Put yourself in the buyer's shoes, and objectively walk through your home as if seeing it for the first time. By viewing your home through this new lens of feng shui, and understanding clutter blocks positive chi, you will see your furnishings and possessions from a new perspective.

Help buyers focus on the best your house has to offer during the initial showing. ***If your home does not grab the buyers' attention on the first visit, chances are they will not be back.*** The clutter-free house attracts and holds the buyers' interest. I have to emphasize this point: as a seller, you have one clear shot at keeping the buyer wanting what you have to offer. The old adage is true: ***You will never get a second chance to make a first impression.***

De-Cluttering the Kitchen — Take It All Off

An old real estate cliché: If the cook falls in love with the kitchen, you are halfway to escrow. In feng shui, the kitchen is of paramount importance and Chinese feng shui practitioners pay special attention to their kitchens. Begin your cleaning in the kitchen by removing *everything* from the counters. Immaculate counter tops impress most cooks and the room itself will feel more spacious with less in it. Ask yourself, what *absolutely* has to remain on the counter? Leave out one or two attractive canisters and the coffeepot. Everything else can go into drawers, the pantry, or better yet, into the box destined for the thrift store.

Do the same to the top of the refrigerator. Place an attractive serving bowl or basket on top. Remove all the do-dads and magnets from the front and sides of the refrigerator, and give the exterior a good cleaning. The kitchen table gets the same treatment — *take it all off*. Put back a simple and attractive centerpiece or bowl of fresh fruit.

Salt and pepper shakers are okay, or a nice candle, but not much more. Resist the temptation to sneak all the stuff back. You are getting ready to move, and the idea is to pare down and simplify your belongings so that a buyer can focus on your home and not all the things inside.

In the kitchen and service areas, all of the following need to disappear: cleaning supplies, brooms, dustpans, sponges, dish soap, and scrub brushes. Garbage and recycling bins are necessities, but not visually appealing. Empty them frequently and put them out of sight. Plastic and paper grocery bags are an eyesore; tuck them away. In the telephone area, place telephone books in a drawer or on a shelf and leave only one pen and a pad of paper visible. Continue this process with all the drawers and cupboards and know that you are making great progress!

Buyers Don't Miss a Thing

In the business of real estate, there is etiquette surrounding what areas of a home are open to examination by a potential buyer during a walk-through. In the kitchen, buyers want to see the depth of storage cupboards and know that the drawers slide easily. The pantry is of special interest. Is the area spacious and the shelving accessible? Even a mildly interested buyer will open doors under the kitchen and bathroom sinks to check for moisture or leaks.

Should a buyer pass these areas by, chances are they will not be making an offer on your home. That is fine since you cannot please everyone, and besides, the reason that a buyer left may be that the floor plan or size did not appeal to him or her. Do not be discouraged.

Remember that you want to capture and hold the attention of every single buyer who *can* work with what your home has to offer, and not let them leave with anything less than a glowing first impression.

Real estate agents try hard to pay attention to what their clients examine during a visit. After well over twenty years in the real estate business, I can say most buyers are respectful and sensitive of someone else's personal space during a visit. They try to be thorough, but not excessively nosy, and they can even be rather shy about being in someone else's home. Often, buyers do not spend *enough* time inspecting what is important when considering a home to purchase.

Bathrooms Need Special Attention

Especially in older homes, bathrooms are usually small and cramped. However, even in the most spacious bathrooms, use the same tactic for clearing clutter as you did with the kitchen — remove everything that makes the room look smaller or crowded. Take off all cosmetic jars, jewelry, and bottles of lotions and potions. Leave only what is absolutely essential and attractive. Leave a great looking perfume bottle, lotion container, or guest hand towel (since a client may ask to use the bathroom while looking at your home!). Be sensitive to the potential buyer when it comes to lingerie left around the bathroom. The last thing a buyer (or an agent) wants to encounter is the dressing area *filled* with personal underclothing. Keep laundry hampers closed and empty the trash containers frequently.

You want the buyers to be impressed at how well you have cared for your home. Buyers tend to associate messy living conditions with a poorly cared for house. Recall that our homes reflect our personal lives, and buyers may think: "If this is the way the owners live, what else about this house has been overlooked and neglected?"

Prospective buyers need to know the condition of the tub and shower and they will open doors and pull back shower curtains for inspection of the interior. Mold indicates poor ventilation and air circulation. Heavy calcium around tub and shower edges indicates exceptionally hard water. Tub enclosure doors are obvious red flag areas for this problem. If water spots and calcium build-up are removed, a buyer realizes that this took extra time, effort, and continual maintenance.

Remember that using feng shui knowledge is not about spending a lot of money on expensive designer towels and fluffy throw rugs. It is about cleanliness, conveying a feeling of order, and regular maintenance. Think of this part of clutter-clearing like germ warfare and go on an all-out campaign to eliminate anything, anywhere, that is dirty and littered with refuse. This concept seems like simple common sense, but displaying these qualities of being tidy and spick-and-span indicates that the home is well cared for, no matter how simple or humble it is. Feng shui is all about homes that *feel* good. Buyers love this immaculate quality about a property, and the subliminal message you create with cleanliness and order will directly affect a buyer's decision about which home to purchase.

Keeping the Good Chi In

According to the ancient design science of feng shui, wherever there are drains in a home, energetically speaking, the benevolent chi energy can be flushed or drained away. This is *not* good feng shui. ***Always keep the toilet lids down*** and close the doors to bathrooms if possible. If closing the door is not practical for ventilation purposes, at least close the bathroom or laundry room door most of the way, and leave it slightly ajar for fresh air to circulate.

A traditional feng shui solution to help the good chi bypass a bathroom is to put a large oval mirror on the outside of the door. A mirror deflects the chi from entering the bathroom and encourages it to keep moving easily and gently throughout the rest of the house. In addition, real estate agents know, from a hygienic and esthetic standpoint, that *bathrooms look much better when the toilet lids are closed.* It may seem like a petty detail, but keep lids *down*.

In Chinese symbolism, water represents abundance, opportunity, and blessings of all kinds, and as a result, most Chinese buyers, or serious feng shui followers; will avoid houses where bathrooms are adjacent to kitchens. The good chi from the all-important kitchen is energetically in conflict with the bathroom and its chi-draining forces. Considered the mouth of chi, the front door of a home ushers in all blessings and good energy flow. It is simply *not* good feng shui to enter a home and immediately view a bathroom, such a private, personal space where good chi drains away. Thus, if your bathroom or powder room is visible from the front entry, or adjacent to the kitchen, keep the bathroom door closed.

It is beyond the scope of this book to explain in depth all the intricacies and applications of feng shui. For the purpose of selling your home, it is helpful to know that in this philosophy (BTB School tradition) the far-left corner of the home is considered to be the Wealth position; while the far-right corner is the Relationships sector. Followers of Compass School feng shui (see Chapter 3) will try to avoid bathrooms in the southeast or Money area (Refer to Appendix A, Compass School Pa kua). None of these locations mentioned are encouraged for a bathroom because favorable chi can be flushed down the drain. I am not suggesting that you relocate plumbing or remodel your floor plan! Since it is impractical to shut off these rooms completely, simply keep the doors closed and use the mirror technique already described.

We Have to Live in the House We're Trying to Sell

Buyers realize that we are still living in our homes while the house is on the market, and they will make allowances for a lived-in look. Even so, coffee tables, end tables, magazine racks, and chairs piled with newspapers and television remote controls are distracting to buyers and need to be orderly and clean

Make a valiant effort at clearing off the dining room table and keeping it that way. The dining room symbolizes the energy and power of family togetherness, and happy times spent around the dinner table. To enhance the look and the feeling of family closeness, place an attractive tablecloth to cover and enhance the surface and soften the sharp edges of table corners. Simple centerpieces and fresh flowers are definite assets. These effective touches will evoke buyers' smiles as they remember your special home.

When you look through decorator magazines at elegantly designed houses, or if you visit an expensive home, something you will *not* see is electric cords. We can take a clue here from feng shui as well as up-scale decorating and do what we can to hide unsightly cords. Visually, cords (especially dark ones against a light wall or carpet) are distracting and unattractive; we have to live with them, *but we do not have to look at them.* Think of creative ways to camouflage cords with plants or attractive baskets, or arrange the furnishings in such a way as to conceal them. In a home-office setting, the maze of computer wiring can be especially difficult to disguise. *Remember that the problem is a visual one, for if they are out of sight, they are no longer energetically distracting.* Often a strategically placed plant, even a silk one in an attractive container, will do the trick. Cords under carpeting can be a hazard. As always, keep safety in mind.

The Nose Knows

Aromas emanating from the rooms in our home, especially the kitchen should be subtle, delicious, and inviting. Before a buyer arrives, think about baking a fresh batch of cookies or heating a little bit of cinnamon in water. I have even heard of a room spray that supposedly smells like freshly baked bread — what a great idea! Aromatherapy works wonders and fragrance candles go a long way toward healing noxious household odors. Avoid any scent that is too

70

sweet or overpowering. Potpourris are very temporary in their effectiveness, soon their aroma fades and quickly they become little bowls of lifeless chi.

Every home has its own particular aromatic essence, but sellers need to be aware of offensive household odors, including noxious pet smells. These are especially unpleasant, and on a warm or damp day they can sabotage a prospective sale. Pet odors, no matter how faint, make it very difficult for many buyers to focus on the otherwise fine qualities of the home. Sellers are encouraged to keep dogs and cats outside if possible when buyers are viewing a home. If pets must be indoors, they should be well groomed and bathed frequently.

Have carpeting professionally cleaned and deodorized. Pet owners become de-sensitized and unaware of animal odors as they live with the aroma on a daily basis. I can tell you as a real estate broker and feng shui consultant, *there are very few things about a home that will sink a seller's ship faster than an offensive pet smell.*

It helps to ask a good friend to be honest and help identify any difficult aromas inside our home. This can be a touchy matter, but a wise seller will tackle the problem. Your best allies are fresh air, sunshine, and professionally cleaned (and deodorized) carpets. A few open windows throughout the house go a long way toward eliminating musty smells, as well as the aroma of last night's fish dinner!

Pets are special and important to us, and their needs must be considered when selling a home. However, keep pet food and containers clean and inconspicuous, preferably outside. If you have indoor cats and dogs with long hair, they pose an additional dilemma. Let's face it, our pets shed their fur, and it flies everywhere; and at certain times of the year it gets worse. Some buyers are particularly allergic to pets and animal dander of any kind. You do not want to lose a sale because your buyer cannot stop sneezing!

When potential buyers are often coming to visit, cleaning up the hair that pets have shed and frequently replacing fresh kitty litter is a must. There is nothing like the odor of a litter box on a warm day — truly unforgettable. Sensitive buyers will have a hard time getting past this smell, and when the showing is over, that may be what they remember most.

If a smoker lives in the house, you should know how thoroughly cigarette and cigar odors penetrate carpeting, draperies, and furnishings. Smoke smell can be so offensive and overwhelming to non-smokers that potential buyers apologize as they bolt for the door to escape. Cigarette smoke is difficult, but not impossible, to eliminate. A new coat of fresh paint and carpet and drapery cleaning accomplish more than making walls and floors look pretty. Cleaning and painting eliminate offensive smells accumulated through years of second-hand smoke. However, before you paint, you will want to pre-wash all the walls. Tri-sodium-phosphate (TSP™ — available at most grocery and hardware stores) removes grease, oils, and smoke build-up. If the problem is especially serious, there are professional services available for *catastrophe cleaning*. They can be found in the yellow pages under "Fire and Water Damage Restoration" and "Property Maintenance." Enlist their services; it may increase the value of your home by thousands of dollars.

When you have accomplished all these tasks, the inside of your home has a fresh new look and a fresh new smell! Also, interior painting requires the removal of everything from the walls. Do not forget, only put back a few, select items. Resist the temptation to rehang the family photographs that lined your hallways. Remember, you are moving.

In feng shui, the windows of a house are considered the eyes of the home through which the outdoors and the loveliness of nature is viewed. In oriental architecture, designers emphasize framing a particular exterior view through each window. The idea is to create an outdoor work of art to be savored and fully appreciated from the interior.

Since a buyer will likely be paying hundreds of thousands of dollars for your home, you are well advised to spend the money to have your windows professionally cleaned, especially in order to bring out any worthwhile or value-enhancing view. Clean windows are almost as good as fresh paint; they make the house sparkle from the inside as well as well as out.

Remember that assessing your home with a feng shui attitude towards cleaning and major clutter-clearing is the first step and it cannot be accomplished overnight. You will need sufficient time to concentrate on each area of your home. Taking the time to assess how your home will feel to a prospective buyer, and implementing the clutter-clearing techniques discussed above before listing your home will give you a quantum boost toward your goal of a rapid sale.

Seller's Checklist for Clearing Clutter

❏ Assess your home objectively. Make a thorough list of what needs attention room by room.

❏ Focus on removing clutter in each room. Ask a friend to help if necessary.

❏ Begin with the kitchen and remove everything from counter tops.

❏ Clean counters well and only put back what is necessary.

❏ Be critical of pet food areas. If possible, keep dishes/bowls outside.

❏ Remove everything from bathroom counter tops. Clean thoroughly. Put only three items back.

❏ Have a clothes hamper with a lid for laundry items.

❏ Hang towels neatly and open a window after showering.

❏ Explain to all family members about keeping toilet lids down.

❏ Keep laundry areas uncluttered. All soaps in cupboards or out of sight.

❏ Have a storage bin for children's toys.

❏ Decide if interior painting is needed. (Pre-wash with TSP™.)

❏ Put the absolute minimum number of pictures back on walls.

❏ Clean off the dining room table. Place fresh flowers or simple centerpiece.

- ❑ Remove all excess clutter, including newspapers and magazines from family and living room areas.

- ❑ Visually camouflage all electric cords.

- ❑ Store away any unnecessary furniture.

- ❑ Keep blinds up for sunshine and several windows slightly open for ventilation.

- ❑ Have all windows washed (professionally, or do this yourself).

- ❑ Have the carpets professionally cleaned and deodorized for smoking, pet odors, or general soil.

5

Transform the Front Yard
and Entryway

"First we shape our homes, and then our homes shape us."

— Winston Churchill

For more than a month, Terry and Sue have been driving around looking at homes for sale. They want a comfortable and well cared for home. Every weekend they search the latest real estate ads, call to get addresses from the listing brokers, and then jump in the car clutching their newspaper with the tempting photos circled. By now, they have the process down to a science: Terry drives while Sue acts as navigator and secretary.

As a writer for a stockbroker trade journal, Terry is admittedly not the handy type. Aware of his limitations, he does not want to buy anything that requires too much work to fix up and maintain. After he finishes an intense writing assignment, all he wants to do is relax, preferably outdoors in the yard. Sue also puts in a tiring day as a high school teacher. Her joy is to be in the garden before preparing dinner. They want to smile as they drive up to their new home each day. Neither of them has the time or energy to fix yard and landscaping problems that already exist; they just want to step in and maintain what someone else has tastefully created.

During Terry and Sue's search for a new home, they have discovered that the condition of the exterior usually indicates the condition of the interior. After all these weeks of looking, just by parking in front of a house, they feel they can size up the whole property based on what the front yard and entry look like. Attractive landscaping, trimmed grass, swept leaves, and an uncluttered porch, usually indicate how these owners have cared for the interior as well. If they see an especially attractive front yard and entry, Sue marks the ad as one to make an appointment to see.

Curb Appeal — The Ace in the Seller's Hand

Real estate agents know from years of experience that curb appeal is powerful. The initial glimpse of your property is the first connection a buyer has with a home, and this impression sets the tone for the rest of the showing. Clients will often tell an agent, "please keep on driving," when they approach a house for sale with a poorly kept front yard. They know this is a big clue as to how the rest of the house has been maintained. They do not want to pay hundreds of thousands of dollars to deal with problems the current owner has ignored.

The Curb Appeal Formula		
The buyer sees:	**The buyer thinks:**	**The buyer decides:**
Weeds in the front yard	Neglected	Forget it!
Dying plants & clutter	Poorly maintained	We don't want it!
Dirty driveway	Unseen problems	Let's go!

Create a Pleasant Pathway to Your Home

In feng shui, pathways are like energetic watercourses. They guide our footsteps as well as our eyes from one point to another. The old saying, "The shortest distance between two points is a straight line," is not always the best choice and does *not* apply in the harmonious and tranquil world of feng shui. Like a powerful riverbed with fast flowing water, straight and direct walkways to the front door bring in the all-important chi too quickly and can create what is called a *sha* element, or an arrow of negative, cutting energy pointing toward the entrance. Consider how an arrow flies… swiftly and straight to its target — it brings injury and pain. Feng shui avoids this type of energetic imagery by altering and softening the trajectory of the arrow with meandering and gently curved pathways.

Curving walkways are especially encouraged in feng shui because a flowing approach to a home lets the chi slow down and enter the dwelling in a more balanced and harmonious way. Thus, the gentle and subtle *yin* energy helps the guest slow down and savor the approach, feeling more welcomed. Straight or angular pathways have more *yang* energy, which send a message of formality, rigidity, and stiffness.

So, use a bit of feng shui magic; balance and soften any rigid lines along the way with meandering plants and round flowerpots blooming with color to diffuse the harsh *sha* energy. Creative placement of these low-cost design balancers will diminish the hard edges and soften the rigidity of brick or concrete walkways.

Your Front Door — the Wondrous *Mouth of Chi*

In feng shui, the portal through which the world enters your home is considered the "mouth of chi" and is one of the most powerful and important aspects of your entire property. Abundance, blessings, opportunities, and good fortune all enter through the front door. The entrance is where buyers and guests experience your house for the first time. *As a seller, you need to pay special attention to this area.*

In Chapter 1 we spoke about how our home is like a mirror that reflects our inner selves. The front door, the mouth of chi, is also a powerful reflection of who you, the seller, are. Because it further indicates how well the rest of the property has been cared for, you want to make it as inviting and pleasant as you possibly can. Use some of the following feng shui techniques and your guests will sense the harmony, balance, simplicity, and serenity that you have created.

Since your entryway is where the buyer takes in the front of your home while the agent gets out the key or waits for you to open the door, let this entrance be *entrancing.* As if you are the buyer, look carefully at your front porch. While your home is for sale, keep this area immaculate and free of leaves and cobwebs; sweep it daily if necessary. Roll up the hose and store it out of sight. Garden tools, gloves, work shoes, etc. add clutter and should disappear. Keep any frequently used equipment handy, but out of view, in an attractive wicker basket or some other covered container close to the porch.

Consider placing an inviting bench or cushioned seating near the entryway. This provides an element of serenity and relaxation for your guests. Not all porches have room for this additional feature, but

80

if yours has some space to spare, suggesting a place to rest will have a desirable effect. Potential buyers might even imagine themselves sitting down and relaxing in the morning or afternoon with their favorite book or newspaper!

In addition to being functional, lighting your entryway and the path leading up to your front porch sets a practical as well as a delightful tone. Feng shui teaches that attractive lighting contributes to comfort and safety as well as aesthetics. These days it is easy and relatively inexpensive to install mood lighting, sometimes called Malibu™ twelve-volt lighting, along the walkway to the front door. Although most of your real estate showings will occur during the day, make sure the porch light hangs straight, operates well, and is clean and free of cobwebs.

Occasionally a buyer may need to visit your home after business hours. This is where your lighting techniques will truly shine. Be sure to place the bulbs so they do not glare in people's eyes. Like a painting hanging out of balance on a wall, crooked or poorly hung light fixtures make some people energetically nervous, and they will want to straighten them. Remember that feng shui is not about spending a lot of money on lavish landscaping, expensive lawn furniture, flowerpots, and costly doorknockers — this is the domain of less is best. Use what you have to its best advantage by clearing, cleaning, and simplifying.

The Not-So-Green Thumb

Although some people have a real knack for gardening, trying to acquire this skill while selling your home may not be a good use of your time. No matter what the color of your thumb, be honest with yourself when it comes to assessing your interior plants and exterior landscaping. If a plant looks forlorn, is yellowing, bug infested, or dying a slow death, bless it and give it back to Mother Earth. You are doing yourself and the plant a favor.

Untended or dying plants are in the same category as peeling paint and cobwebs; they are signs of neglect. If a plant has bugs, try spraying it with soapy water. For stubborn leaf or stem scale, gently remove the offenders using a cotton ball or a cotton swab with a bit of sesame oil. Dead and dying plants symbolize dead chi, which is the opposite of what feng shui is designed to surround us with — vibrant, lush plant life and healthy energy of all kinds.

It will pay you good dividends to put a lot of your energy into making the front porch particularly attractive. Avoid spiny cactus and sharp or spiked-leafed plants. Those make a buyer shrink back and not feel welcome on an energetic level. Instead, concentrate on leaves with round and gentle shapes such as *ficus benjimina* and *schiffelera*.

Colorful bowls of bedding plants with a variety of blooming flowers are inexpensive and can be found at most garden shops, nurseries, or even large pharmacies. For about ten dollars, you can purchase lovely pots filled with a variety of brightly colored plants. Flowers such as pink impatiens, yellow and blue pansies, scarlet and purple petunias, white sweet alyssum, and cobalt blue lobelia are a few suggestions. They will create a definite welcoming effect at your doorway. Keep them watered and pick off dead or dying blossoms regularly.

Place pots of blooming flowers in groupings of three or five and varying in arrangements from large to small (odd numbers of elements are more interesting, and artists often use this design technique). Without overcrowding the porch, splurge here and do not skimp with the blooming flowers. With good care, this small but important investment should last through the close of escrow!

Bring Out the Welcome Mat

Most homes have a doormat at the front entry. You want the one on your porch to look clean and fresh. Shake the mat out well and sweep underneath. Remove any dead leaves and dirt deposited from months of daily foot traffic. Mats with cute sayings or cartoons of farm animals might be humorous or clever another time, but while you are selling your home, they simply detract from the natural, harmonious feeling you are trying to create.

If you decide to buy a new mat, use this feng shui tip: since our doors have 90 degree angles, often inset with more rectangular panels, an *oval or round* doormat will bring the entry into better equilibrium. This subtle design distinction goes back to balancing the qualities of the *yang* corners with the *yin* rounded edges, thus enhancing the effect of energetic serenity.

From a Distance

Your home's numbers must be easy to see and readable from the street. Walk out to the front curb and carefully assess your address. If your numbers are hidden or even partially obstructed by vines or plants of any kind, how can the world and abundant energy find you? How could the fire department or emergency vehicles bring help or assistance? Common sense tells us to announce our home to those who seek us with large and tasteful numbers.

Sometimes the house numbers are painted on street curbs or placed on mailboxes at the front of the yard. Either technique is helpful and encouraged. Why keep people guessing and have them driving up and down the street looking for your home? If needed, repaint the numbers wherever they appear. Make them fresh, clear, and readable from afar — especially from across the street.

Turn on the Water

Often the main entry is centered at the front of the house. In BTB feng shui, this center front area represents our Career Life Sector (See Appendix B) and its element is water — the blessing that comes from heaven. Recognizing that water symbolizes abundance in all aspects of our lives, a water feature in the entryway of our home creates exceptionally good feng shui.

A simple fountain, either outside the front door or just within the interior entryway, is an excellent way to greet guests or welcome you home. The sight and sound of clear, gently moving water has a calming effect on the human spirit. Evoking images of a babbling brook helps bring peace and tranquility to the mind and soul.

For good fortune, feng shui recommends having the flow of the water pointing toward the front door. Keep the water level of the fountain full and ensure that it is clean and sparkling with a drop or two of chlorine every few weeks. Occasionally, you will need to clean calcium residue with a lime remover solution and a cloth. While the real estate agent retrieves the key from the lockbox or waits for you to answer the door, the serene sight and sound of the fountain will help those few moments pass more easily. Buyers will feel refreshed, relaxed, and welcomed into your special home.

Sentinels on Your Doorstep

Often feng shui practitioners will position a pair of guardians at the entrance; they put one on each side of the front porch or at the bottom of steps leading up to the main door. Think of the *fu dogs* (the grinning dog-like guardians often seen in front of Asian establishments on either side of the front portal) or lions that protect the entrance to impressive buildings such as palaces, banks, and hotels. This sentinel element is very important because it symbolically turns away negative energy from the dwelling or business. It helps if these porch guardians look solid and firm, yet friendly!

Homeowners, if they would like, can apply this same idea to residences by simply placing a bowl of colorful flowers on either side of the front door. Further enhancing your porch area, matching urns with soft ferns or plants with vibrant color can accomplish the same thing. Many nurseries carry stone or cast figures of angels or other protective symbols. If this concept appeals to you, explore it further and see if you like the idea of guardians at your entry.

Mirrors — the *Aspirin* of Feng Shui

When sha energy of any kind needs to be deflected or turned away, feng shui practitioners will often use a mirror or reflective surface of some kind. Often referred to as *the aspirin of feng shui*, mirrors are considered powerful tools that operate on an energetic level. In the Chinatowns of San Francisco and many other large cities, small, eight-sided, decorative elements with a circular mirror in the center hang above the front doors of apartment buildings, homes, restaurants, and offices for this purpose.

Called a *Bagua* mirror (or *pa kua* in Compass School), this is the traditional cure for anything energetically negative that might be coming toward the structure and considered threatening in any way. They are *always* hung outside and are usually found above the front door. Bagua mirrors deflect sha energy from a pointed roofline or an upset neighbor from across the street. They also deflect the energy of excess traffic or headlights aimed directly at the house. For thousands of years, this octagonal mirrored device has been used throughout mainland China for feng shui purposes, only driven underground during Chairman Mao's period of influence. Hong Kong, never subject to Mao's system of purging feng shui from the people's thinking, has a thriving feng shui following to this day. You can even sign up to take a Feng Shui Tour of the city from your hotel!

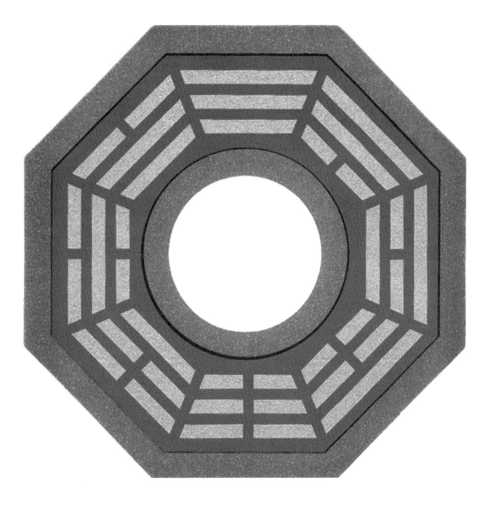

Bagua Mirror

Mirrors, on a subtle level, tell the negative chi to "go back to where it came from." They deflect this sha energy and encourage it to have no effect on this dwelling. Whether you subscribe to this fundamental aspect of feng shui thinking or not, protecting your front door in a physical sense is a good idea. Traditional Western protectors might be wrought iron gates, retaining walls, or shrubbery that buffer the property from the noisy street, giving a feeling of increased privacy and security.

Homes at the top or bulb of a cul-de-sac are prone to a constant stream of headlights, and traffic points directly at them whenever a car enters the street; this top position absorbs all traffic energy. To deflect this sha chi, carefully place dense shrubs, hedges, sentinel trees, retaining walls, or gates. Be sure not to position trees too close to, or directly in front of the main door. This would block the good chi from entering the dwelling.

Seller's Feng Shui Entry & Porch Checklist

❑ Assess your front yard and entryway from the street. Make a list of what needs attention.

❑ If your front path is straight or angular, soften it with plants having round shapes and leaves.

❑ Thoroughly clean and, if needed, paint or re-varnish your front door. Clean all glass windows and doors. Oil squeaky hinges.

❑ If you have a front screen door, make certain it is clean. If it shows signs of age or rust, give it a fresh coat of enamel paint or replace it. Be sure it does not clip a guest in the back of the ankle. Not good feng shui!

❑ Sweep the steps and clean under the doormat. Replace worn doormats.

❑ Remove all cobwebs from the entry and anywhere around the front of the house.

- ❑ Check the handle or doorknob to ensure it is easy to grasp, feels solid, and does not stick.

- ❑ Repair it if it needs attention. If it is made of brass, give it a shine.

- ❑ Be sure the key for real estate agents fits smoothly in the keyhole and is easy to use. If there is more than one key, label them.

- ❑ Examine the threshold and be certain it is solid, fastened securely, and does not wobble.

- ❑ Put fresh pots of cheerful, blooming flowers on the porch.

- ❑ Use round pots instead of pots with sharp edges and corners.

- ❑ Remove any dead plants or bushes with thorny leaves. Cut back anything that is scratchy, uncomfortable, or unwelcoming to the touch.

- ❑ Consider where you might place a simple fountain. Be sure the water flows *toward* the front door. Direct the good energy in and not away from the dwelling.

- ❑ Have a functioning doorbell with a pleasant ring, not an irritating buzz.

- ❑ Inspect your porch light and make sure it is clean, working, and hanging straight.

- ❑ Make sure the house address number is easy to find and readable from a distance.

6

Feng Shui Magic
Room by Room

"One's mind, once stretched by a new idea, never regains its original dimensions."

— Oliver Wendell Holmes

Jackie and Kevin tried for several months to find their dream home. They were looking for a well-designed floor plan that would work for their busy lifestyle. They were willing to do some sprucing up, but they needed adequate room for entertaining and frequent overnight guests. One day their agent took them to a property she described as "just what they wanted."

The owner greeted them and then went into the back yard while they went through the home. Upon entering, they smelled fresh cookies baking and Jackie smiled as she noticed the welcoming fountain in the entryway. The house was not grand, yet it had a simple elegance and style. A large mirror hanging in the small entry seemed to double the space and light.

In the cozy living room, Kevin noted the built-in bookcase that would be perfect for their large library. The few unobtrusive wall hangings did not distract the eye from a view of the side yard and flower garden through the crystal-clear bay window. Although the room was not as large as they desired, the furniture framed the fireplace and encouraged conversation; they could imagine how their own sofa, chairs, and coffee table would look there. Fresh flowers on the dining room table, glowing hardwood floors, and an oval mirror reflecting the hanging baskets of flowers outside, all made Jackie comment "This home just feels good."

Opening the compact and well-organized kitchen pantry, Jackie knew the kitchen would work for her. The room was light, sunny, and inviting with immaculate counters and older, but spotless, appliances. The storage cupboards were accessible and well-designed. Kevin looked under the sink and pronounced it dry and large enough to accommodate the reverse-osmosis system he wanted to install.

A long hallway led to the bedrooms in the back of the home. Normally, this space would have been dark and gloomy, but the owners had installed a skylight in the hallway that flooded the area with light. Hanging beneath the skylight was a delightful mobile of crystal butterflies that danced with the air coming in through an open window in one of the bedrooms. On the far wall, another mirror captured the light and reflected it into the two sleeping areas on either side.

The master bedroom was in the far right corner of the home and had a French door that opened onto a private patio filled with ferns and flowers. They felt as if they had entered a sanctuary. Jackie commented on how much she liked the bed placed diagonally into the corner farthest from the doorway. Because this was an older house, the bedrooms were small, but both Jackie and Kevin were ready to pare down, simplify, and get rid of some of their bulky furniture.

The bathrooms were Spartan but sparkling, especially the tile, cupboards, sinks, and tub areas. More fresh flowers were on the counters, and their fragrance filled the small space. After checking for leaky plumbing or crumbling plaster, Kevin told Jackie how well this home had been cared for.

On the way to the garage they passed through the laundry room where everything was neatly stored in the overhead cupboards; there was even a hanging bar in place for drying clothes. Even though there was no workbench in the garage, Kevin saw the extra shelving and how orderly and clean everything was. He felt that the space in one corner gave him room to build his own workbench.

In the back yard, they noticed the simple yet attractive landscaping, with all the garden tools and yard equipment neatly stored in a small shed. The patio furniture was placed in a shaded area surrounded by colorful plants, and they could hear the sound of flowing water from the fountain that was nestled between two large ferns. Jackie saw space for an herb garden.

The home was smaller and older than they wanted, but everything was in excellent condition. This was very important to Kevin because, though he was handy, he didn't have the time or the inclination to fix up a place that had been neglected. Jackie especially loved the inviting master bedroom and the sunny kitchen. Deciding that this was the right house for them, they drove back to the office to write an offer.

The Entryway

We've talked earlier about buyers liking homes that feel good and how your doorway is their first point of significant contact with your home. To get the showing (and the good feelings) off to a great start, keep your entry as light, spacious, and immaculate as possible. The front door should allow guests to graciously enter into your personal world. As feng shui is practiced in China, front doors are often painted red or outlined in this auspicious color. However, you do not have to paint your door red to have good feng shui. If red does not appeal to you, or is inappropriate to your design, just be sure that the paint or varnish looks fresh. The colors black, deep green, dark blue, or natural wood are also good feng shui selections for front doors.

Remove "No Solicitors" signs. This is a subtle message to a buyer that you have too many salespeople coming through your neighborhood and does not send a welcoming signal to anyone. Bars on windows or obvious window decals or signs advertising a security system are also questionable at this time. They serve to alert a buyer that the neighborhood needs extra protection. However, if your neighborhood requires that your home have extra security, leave your protective devices in place. Just make sure they look clean and that bars over windows are not rusted.

The all-important front door should open as fully as possible and not be hindered by objects such as furniture, toys, boxes, or plants. According to feng shui principles, if your mouth of chi does not open fully, then abundance and new opportunities cannot enter easily. The entry area is a perfect place for fresh flowers. Whatever the eye first falls on after entering the home should be as beautiful and serene as possible, as this subtly sets the tone of the whole home.

As discussed earlier, in feng shui, water represents abundance and fortunate blessings. So a fountain of fresh moving water near the entry is especially appropriate. The welcoming sound will relieve tension and put visitors and buyers into a serene frame of mind, ready to appreciate your home and enjoy the stage you have carefully set.

While proceeding into the next room, clear away any furniture that might block the flow of chi as well as the buyer's progress. People should be able to move forward easily and without obstruction into the inviting space you have created. Move or remove any item that is in the way. When selling your home, think: Less is more.

You might even give some thought to having a shoeless home. A bench or a low shelf near the front door invites guests to leave their footwear. Next to the bench, place a simple and attractive wicker basket with cuddly socks or easily washable booties (like the kind you receive on long flights). Shoe-free homes are especially appropriate when the carpeting is a light color or if buyers and agents will be coming through your home in wet weather.

At first, some people might feel inconvenienced removing their shoes, but on a deeper level it shows that you honor your home in a special way. In upscale homes, with expensive carpeting, a gentle request to clients and agents to remove their shoes is not out of line. However, if a shoe-free home doesn't appeal to you, or if your home is so informal that shoe-removal would be entirely out of place, don't use this technique as a pretense. That would surely backfire.

The Living Room and Family Room

Some living rooms convey just the opposite feeling — they appear so formal even the Avon lady would feel uncomfortable. Formality may have been attractive in the 1950's, but it is totally out of place with today's casual lifestyles. Symmetrical design has its place, but buyers will feel much more relaxed in a setting that is less rigid and more inviting. If your sofa or other furniture has angular corners, drape a shawl over an edge and let it cascade over the cushions and seating space. This is a softening *yin* treatment for a hard *yang* element. Try using tablecloths over dining room and coffee tables with pointy corners. The effect immediately softens the energetically offensive hard edges.

Look at how your window coverings appear from the street and front walkway. Be sure they hang straight, without sagging hemlines, water stains, or missing hooks. Replace broken shades or bent mini-blinds. Arrange living room furniture in intimate groupings to stimulate conversation. For coffee and snacks, place low tables conveniently but not in the way of easy movement throughout the room. Furnishings spaced too far apart separate and isolate people. Feng shui encourages us to draw people together, yet allows for privacy when desired.

In homes with a family room that is separate from the living room, buyers understand that this family area is more relaxed and casual, and therefore looks more lived in than the living room. However, all the above rules would still apply — it does not mean that any clutter or areas of stuck chi are okay. *You still want to convey a sense of order within the informality.* Look at your family room critically and remove unnecessary items. It is very easy to overlook piles of books, magazines, and newspapers here because this is where you tell yourself: I'll get to it later.

The Dining Room

In many homes the dining room needs to be reclaimed for its intended purpose. We learn in feng shui that each space has a function for which it was designed and that is its highest and best use. To disregard this original function and design intention energetically puts the room *out of balance.* Especially when selling your house, you will want to show off your dining space at its finest.

Use an immaculate tablecloth or attractive placemats, or if your table surface is especially handsome, let it shine unencumbered. Fresh flowers, a fruit bowl, or candles are the only things that need to be on the table. Remove excess furniture, and make the space as open and inviting as possible. On a wall near the table, consider hanging a large mirror. If your table is round, use a rectangular mirror; if your table has pointed corners, balance this shape with an oval mirror. Mirrors serve to visually as well as energetically double the abundance of food and whatever else is on the table. You will notice most Chinese restaurants use lots of mirrors!

If there is a pleasant view from any of the dining room windows, a large mirror will multiply the view. *If there is a broken mirror anywhere in the home, remove or replace it.* In feng shui, mirrors are very important *amplifiers of energy* and abundance. A broken mirror is similar to a computer that doesn't work; it creates energetic havoc and frustration, distorting the good energy that would normally be present.

The Master Bedroom —
Rest, Romance, and Relaxation

We spend one-third of our lives in the master bedroom, a very important feng shui room. Ideally located at the quiet rear of the house, this sleeping space provides the owner with the gentle *yin* energy of rest, romance, and relaxation. Feng shui encourages the removal of any decorative items or furnishings that do not further these goals (such as filing cabinets and office equipment).

If the master bedroom is located in the far right corner from the entrance, or in the southwest quadrant of the house, so much the better! As mentioned earlier, feng shui considers this area the Relationships sector (see Appendix B). Accordingly, floor plans with this layout are considered to be especially auspicious in solidifying the long-term relationship and romance of the owners. Followers of feng shui will find this design very appealing.

Decorating colors for the master bedroom area can be restful, yin hues that promote serenity, relaxation, and romance, such as soft tones of green, blue, and lavender. Artful accents such as candles, pictures, or artwork in shades of pink, the color specific to the Relationships sector of the feng shui *Bagua* (see Appendix B), will add spice to your life and fire to your romance! An old feng shui tradition advises against using a peach hue in the master bedroom. This color's unhappy energy supposedly brings *peach-blossom luck,* which suggests that the loved one will be unfaithful.

During the sale of your home, keep the master bedroom in especially good order with a window open for ventilation. For a spacious feeling, remove most of your personal photos and mementos from dressers and bookcases, leaving only a few to make the room feel homey and happy. Spend time making the master closet orderly and as roomy as possible, since buyers will try to visualize their own things in the closet.

The Feng Shui Command Seating Position

Westerners do not place great emphasis on where we sit or sleep in a room. Asian design, however, incorporates the concept of the *command* or *power position* for furniture placement. The most important person in the room is given the most protected seat that "commands the door." This means that the place of honor, power, and protection is farthest from, and facing toward the entryway of that particular room.

Feng shui teaches that the foot of the bed (in any bedroom) should not point directly out the door because that is how the dead are carried out. If possible, put the master bed in the *command position,* facing the doorway from the farthest corner of the room. If the bed can be placed *diagonally* in this corner, so much the better.

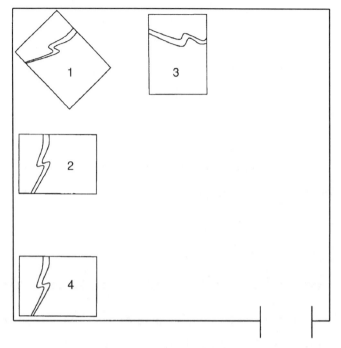

Good Feng Shui Bed Placement

If this arrangement is not possible or does not appeal to you, another option is to hang a mirror in such a way as to reflect the entrance from the chair or bed where the owner prefers to sit or sleep. This gives that position at least a peripheral view of the door. Locating furniture with power in mind is very effective in the master bedroom, the office, the living room, and the dining area when you want to take charge and energetically feel protected and in control. (Try using this technique in your business!)

When buyers see this kind of furniture positioning, they will probably not be consciously aware of the effect. However, on an inner level, it removes the random, haphazard feel to furniture placement in a room and subtly raises the arrangement to one with purpose and clear intention. This energetic distinction *feels* better. When we sit or sleep in the *command position*, we have an inner awareness of both comfort and security.

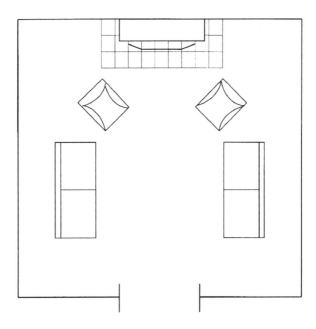

Example of Feng Shui Placement Allowing Chi to Circulate Freely.
(Note the octagonal orientation of seating positions to correspond with the Bagua.)

The Kitchen and Laundry Areas

Feng shui philosophy considers the kitchen to be the most important room in the house. It is the center of home and hearth — where good things happen! Here guests gather during a party, and the cook prepares delicious food to express their love for the family. After you have followed the suggestions from Chapter 4 to de-clutter and clean the kitchen, there are several more feng shui tips to provide further energetic assistance to help sell your house.

Where the cook is happy, there is good feng shui, and a buyer who especially enjoys cooking, will appreciate that the workspace is immaculate, spacious, and as well lighted as possible. In many Chinese kitchens, if the stove is against a wall so the cook's back is to the doorway, they might position a mirror or reflective surface of some kind above the burners on the stove. This symbolically doubles the food being prepared, signifying abundance, and permits the cook to see behind her or him and thus feel more relaxed.

Feng shui in the kitchen begins and ends with cleanliness, and prospective buyers pick up on this during a showing. After you have cleared the clutter, roll up your sleeves and scrub counters and appliance surfaces until they glisten. It is not considered good feng shui to see your kitchen (especially the refrigerator) from the front door or entryway. If this is the situation with your floor plan, you will want to creatively block this view. Keep the door between the kitchen and entry closed, or use a visual element such as a vase or basket of flowers to visually separate the refrigerator from the front door.

Followers of feng shui are alert to this design situation and feel that people first think about going to the kitchen for food when coming home. It is felt that the occupants may then be overweight or have other problems associated with continual weight gain. A feng shui *cure* for this design challenge would be to hang a faceted crystal in the kitchen between the doorway and the refrigerator to deflect the chi thus creating an energetic barrier to the craving of food.

As mentioned earlier, energetically a bathroom should not be adjacent to the kitchen because the bathroom drains jeopardize the feng shui abundance potential of the kitchen; bathrooms are areas where chi is flushed away. If your floor plan has a kitchen adjacent to a bathroom, keep the door between them closed. Placing a mirror on the outside of the door allows the good chi from the kitchen to pass by this negative energetic space and not threaten the benevolent energy of the cooking area.

Laundry areas in the main home are often entered from the garage and can be a secondary mouth of chi. Again, make that entrance attractive and welcoming to a buyer by keeping it clean and uncluttered. Place laundry in covered bins until ready to go into the washer, and keep supplies out of sight in overhead cupboards. (If you don't have any, install some). Make this room pleasant and not a constant reminder of work to be done. From a feng shui standpoint, a washing machine is a large drain of chi. Always keep the lid down and, if possible, conceal the washer and dryer behind attractive curtains or a closet door.

You can decorate the laundry space with an attractive plant on a windowsill, a crystal or a sun catcher in the window, and a pleasant window covering instead of an ordinary mini-blind. Since this room can have a damp feeling, keep a nearby window opened slightly for fresh air. Have the lighting appropriate to the space and perhaps splurge with a decorative light fixture that makes you (and the buyer) smile as you enter the room.

Teen Bedrooms

Just like everyone else, teens need their own space and privacy while the family home is being sold. However, they are old enough to understand that their help and cooperation is vital to getting the best price for the house. A buyer will need to see their rooms and closets, if only briefly, for size and orientation.

The room needs to be clean and pleasant. Questionable posters, negative artwork, and angry images of all kinds need to be removed. Clothes on the floor, a messy desk, or an unmade bed will detract from the overall positive energy of the rest of the home. Teens usually understand exactly what the family is going through during this transition from one home to another. They are hopefully able to step into their highest selves to help parents who are coping with the financial and emotional burden of a family move.

I have found that when young adults are *brought fully into the planning process* and treated as adults, including the decision to sell the family home in the first place, they are far more likely to cooperate. When they understand that their private space is like a mirror of themselves and reflects energetically, positively or negatively, what they are like on the inside, things can take on a new perspective. Of course, adults must provide good models, and teens need to be treated respectfully.

Take the time to talk to the young people in your home and let them know how important their help and cooperation is while the house is being shown to others. They may be the one who answers the phone when the real estate agent calls, or they may be the person who opens the front door to the potential buyer. They need to understand what to do and how to act at these times, as well as how to take care of the family pets when real estate guests come. *Their adult behavior during this time is to be cultivated and expected.*

It would be great if all teenagers were helpful out of an altruistic heart. However, if that quality has not completely developed yet, consider alternatives. Reward them for cooperative and helpful behavior with a movie, dinner out, or concert tickets. Be creative and try to have fun together during this time.

Subtle Feng Shui Design Tips

For the purpose of selling your home, keep any artwork, prints, or paintings *neutral*. Landscapes, seascapes, and still lifes are all good choices. Prints from music festivals, cultural exhibits, and museums will usually send a pleasant energetic message. Take down any pictures depicting sadness or violence, or those containing harsh vivid colors or questionable images of any kind. Visual signals are powerful, so during the time your home is on the market, you want to convey images that are happy and serene to your real estate guests.

Dried floral arrangements used to be prominent in decorating. However, energetically, bouquets of preserved flowers are actually bundles of *lifeless* chi. They simply do not inspire our spirits with the potent energy of living plants. Use them sparingly, if at all. If you must keep them for sentimental reasons, keep them looking vibrant and well dusted. An exception to this rule to not show off dried flowers would be a memento from a special occasion, such as a prom or birthday corsage. However, for selling purposes, these are best removed and boxed for your new house.

Electronic equipment of any kind such as a computer, fax or copy machine, are considered to be high-energy sources in feng shui. Gauss meters indicate that these devices also emit strong electromagnetic frequencies (EMFs) of varying degrees, and are thus *yang* or forceful power centers. If your living room has a television set or a computer, try to enclose it behind cupboard doors in an entertainment center or covered desk area. Some people will artfully mask electronic equipment with silk or another easily draped material. This is better than constantly being visually confronted with the big black box of a television or computer station.

Electronic equipment associated with business or schoolwork is best kept in an office or study, if space permits. It is not a good idea to have this kind of equipment in a living or family room, and *especially* not in a master bedroom. Often, however, when we don't have the luxury of these choices and our space is very limited, living rooms (or even master bedrooms) end up doing double duty. When a living room is required to serve more than one function, try putting the office equipment behind a decorative screen to remove it visually and energetically, or try draping it with an attractive piece of fabric.

Sheltering this electronic equipment from view brings the living room back into balance and allows the space to perform the function for which it was intended — entertaining guests and relaxing. When someone needs to use the desk area and computer, it is easy to move the screen or fabric out of the way. When selling your home, if buyers see that a room is being used for more than one purpose, it sends the message of cramped quarters and that the house doesn't have enough space for everyday living. You want to create the *opposite* effect.

Feng Shui Treatment of Stairways, Doors, and Beams

In feng shui, stairways are like waterfalls; the chi energy like water, goes quickly down, down, down, and is gone. Floor plans with staircases positioned directly facing the all-important front entrance are strongly discouraged. All the abundance, fortunate blessings, and benevolent energy from the top floor of the home, rushes down the stairs and out the front door.

The same is true with energy *coming in* from the main entrance. The chi wants to rush up the stairs, instead of circulating gently on the main floor. This rush of energy is felt on a subtle level, often unconsciously. Many Asian buyers will not consider buying a home with this type of stairway placement.

An energetic cure for this feng shui design problem is to hang an attractive crystal or perhaps a beautiful chandelier over the area where the stairs stop in the foyer. This serves to divert the rushing chi, slow it down, and direct it away from the doorway. Depending on your décor, a ceiling fan can accomplish the same thing. The idea is to hang an *energetic dispersing object* in such a way as to block the chi from escaping. A round or oval area rug at the base of the stairs can also act to hold and circulate the energy and avoid this difficult stairway syndrome.

Spiral staircases are like a corkscrew of downward chi and are a definite feng shui challenge. A remedy would be to place a large, healthy plant under the staircase (silk if necessary) to block the chi from its continuing downward spiral path. More help would be to wind a bower of silk ivy leaves up the rungs of the handrail. Do this in such a way so as not to compromise holding the handrail, but to energetically lift the chi. Stairs with open risers allow energy to fall through. Here again a large plant positioned under the stairway serves to hold the chi and stop the energetic drain.

In feng shui, doors throughout the home are symbolic of the *voices of the adults*, while the windows represent the *voices of the children*. It is best to have doors that open freely and widely into the expanse of the room, instead of into a short or narrow wall. A door that only opens partway does not permit all of the abundance and good chi to enter. You'll want to remove any obstacles that keep all doors from opening fully.

Also, the positioning of doors is important, since it is inauspicious to have doors that bump into each other; in feng shui these are called *arguing doors*. Floor plans that have this door arrangement can benefit from hanging a faceted crystal or a wind chime where the two doors normally would bump into each other. This will deflect the negative chi. On a practical level, try to keep these doors closed whenever possible and only open one of them at a time.

When a front and back door are aligned opposite each other (where you can see the back door from the front door) in a straight path, the chi wants to rush out the rear, especially if the back door is visible from the front entryway. This is often the case in our Western home design when we have French or glass sliding doors that open onto a patio that is visible from the front door. Energetically the chi goes in one door and out the other with no chance to meander gently and work its way through the home. To slow the chi down and to prevent it from rushing out, try placing a potted plant, such as a fern, just in front of the French doors going outside. Another solution to this energetic challenge is to position a coffee table with a floral arrangement or other design element between the two doors. This retains the pleasant view through the glass doors, yet allows the chi to flow around it and circulate within the room itself instead of going straight out the back door.

In a hallway, doors into bedrooms, bathrooms, or office rooms should be evenly spaced across from each other and not be staggered or offset across the hall. Hanging a crystal in the hallway opposite the doors in question can offset the unbalanced energy of doors that have this staggered positioning. Hanging a crystal will deflect and disarm the negative chi coming from the misaligned doorways.

Many of our homes have overhead beams, often decorative and frequently structural. Either way, in feng shui, beams are energetic weights bearing down oppressively on the occupants of a home in a subtle way, especially if they are painted or stained a dark color. To alleviate this heavy, downward-bearing energy, paint the beams white or a light color that matches the ceiling — thus making them disappear into the ceiling, both in a design and an energetic sense.

Overhead beams can emit negative or sha energy in the master bedroom, especially when placed over the bed, over the dining room table, and over the homeowner's seat in the family or living room. Another area where a heavy beam would be unwise is in a room used as an office where the owner spends a great deal of time, especially if the beam crosses over the chair and desk area of the occupant. This is a subtle, energetic effect, but powerful nonetheless, and traditional feng shui would offset this effect by hanging a pair of bamboo flutes facing each other, diagonally on the beam. This ancient cure serves to raise the chi of the beam and to remove the energetic weight from those who sit or sleep below. Bamboo flutes may not fit into your interior decorating, but just be aware of dark overhead beams, and consider painting them a lighter color!

7

Enhance Your Garage, Deck, and Patio

"Do what you can, with what you have, with where you are."

— Theodore Roosevelt

Karin was at her wit's end. As she looked into her garage from the kitchen, she felt the beginning of panic. The idea of sorting through the accumulation of things stored from 30 years of raising children, along with many of her late husband's things that she was not yet willing to part with, was overwhelming. She knew the time had come to clean the garage.

Clearing the garage was vital because she had decided to move into a smaller house. Her two sons were independent and had their own families, so she had to get all their things packed and stored with them. Bill had died seven years ago, and she knew her boys would want some of his things. She called each of them to come and take what they could use and help her go through the rest. This step alone made her feel better.

Her good friends, Anna and Judith, were coming over Sunday to sort through whatever was left. She grinned at the thought of an empty garage by Monday! She had put this off for years and now was ready to get on with it. With the garage cleaned up, she would have a lot more energy to focus on the rest of the house. She called the thrift store and scheduled a pickup for

Monday morning. Her friend, Jack, would come with his truck that afternoon to collect what was headed for the dump.

Her goal was to put the house on the market by the end of the month. Barbara, her real estate agent, had already prepared an informational flyer, and together they brainstormed about what else to do in the rest of the house before putting it up for sale. Karin's excitement grew! She was making progress, and she was not alone in the process.

Time to Roll up Your Sleeves

Homebuyers certainly like nice kitchens; however, when they look at garages they imagine themselves enjoying a hobby, relaxing, puttering, and building projects in their spare time. To most men and a growing number of women, a great garage is a big selling point — *if* it is in good shape. Some spaces in a house are more of a feng shui challenge than others. If your garage is one of these, it is still possible to work with, so don't be discouraged. The garage usually becomes the home's catch-all for the things people do not have another place for. Those things usually sit in never-never land where they are often *never* seen and *never* used again.

Long before the For Sale sign is placed in the front yard, one of the biggest tasks facing most property owners is tackling the disarray of the typical garage. To assess the condition of yours, step into it using your feng shui eyes and take an objective look around. *This is what your buyers will see.* Is this the impression you want to give the people whom you hope to convince to spend hundreds of thousands of dollars to buy your property?

Even though a buyer knows all the stuff in a garage belongs to the owner and it will be gone at the close of escrow, just looking at it in its present, disorganized state is a visual turnoff. This condition is an energetic impediment to the buyer who sees and *feels* the disorder on an internal, subtle level and makes judgments accordingly. So, take a hard look at your garage. If it is filled to the brim with boxes, bags of old clothes, newspapers, old tires, and heaps of odds and ends, it is time to get busy!

The ancient Chinese obviously did not need all that parking and storage space, yet garages are a definite and undeniable part of modern life. Unfortunately for us, most garages have become large residential warehouses and not spaces for parking a car or two. Used not only to store vehicles (whether they run or not), garages have also become laundromats, workshops, and the resting-place of last resort for everything else we do not know what to do with.

How Does Your Garage Rate? Checklist

❑ Do both cars fit easily?

❑ Is the workbench organized?

❑ Are tools neatly arranged?

❑ Is the laundry area tidy with detergents etc. out of sight (if applicable)?

- [ ] Are light fixtures clean and any fluorescent tubes not giving off a humming sound?

- [ ] Are cobwebs removed?

- [ ] Are all window coverings clean or dusted?

- [ ] Are the windows clean (Yes, even in the garage!) and windowsills dusted?

If the above description fits your garage, you get a feng shui gold star!

Some garages have also been converted into offices, family rooms, bedrooms, or recreation spaces with billiard tables or exercise equipment. Consequently, people end up parking their vehicles in the driveway or on the street and not in the area where they were intended. This results in the problem of *inappropriate use of space* since the area does not function as originally intended and is therefore out of feng shui balance.

Parking cars in the driveway and on the street in front of a house can make a property look much less attractive. Buyers who drive by and see many vehicles conclude that the house and garage are not large enough to meet their needs. While your property is for sale, park those extra vehicles elsewhere, perhaps at a friend's home, at work, or your church parking lot (with permission of course!). You want to create an impression of sufficient space for both the family and its automobiles.

If you have modified the structure of your garage (with a wall or room divider), a buyer may request, in their offer to purchase, that a garage conversion be returned to its original condition, especially if the work was done without a city building permit. If this situation arises during the negotiations, be flexible and remember that what works for one person does not necessarily work for another. You may think your bonus room in the garage is great, but it might not appeal to the buyer who otherwise loves your house. Do not let this become a deal breaker.

After eliminating the excess from your garage, your next task is to **temporarily** rent a storage unit. ***A storage unit is the best gift you can give yourself while in the moving process.*** Remember that you are moving anyway and removing some of your excess furnishings will help show your home's best advantages. Yes, this is a brief financial investment, but the rewards it pays include a more spacious home and yard, breathing room to sort through and part with all your extra things, and a clean garage! Good results for a few dollars a day! After you move in and settle down in your new home, if you did a good, thorough job of clutter-clearing, *you will not need this storage unit.*

Moving with a Little Help from Friends

Clearing and cleaning your garage can be an enormous job, so get help from a friend or family member who is organized, energetic, talented, and willing. You can repay them for this gracious gift of their time and energy by reciprocating and offering to help them with an equally difficult task at their home. Once you have found your helper, follow this strategy:

"How to Clear your Garage" Checklist

❑ Get a good night's sleep, put on comfortable shoes and loose clothing.

❑ Start as early in the day as possible.

❑ Have a fresh pot of coffee or green tea already brewed. The idea is, once you get going, you do not want to stop to do little things that will break your stride.

❑ Put on your favorite music to get you going and keep you moving!

❑ Have on hand sufficient boxes, heavy black marking pens, and a supply of large trash bags. Try not to go out and find or buy anything once you have started working.

❑ If at all possible, work with the garage door open. Besides the better light and fresh air, you can easily use the driveway for sorting items that will go to the trash, to the dump, or to the thrift store.

❑ Order a take-out lunch and have it delivered to avoid losing energy or momentum.

❑ Set aside a space where you can place things that will be taken to a thrift store. Recycle whenever possible and *give away what no longer serves you.*

❑ Large landscaping trash bags are strong and can hold a multitude of things that must definitely be tossed. Caution: be extremely careful about throwing away old paint cans, garden chemicals, ant sprays, automotive solvents, etc. **These are considered *hazardous*** *waste* **and must not go to a landfill or your regular trash containers!**

❑ Your telephone book lists numbers for proper waste disposal. You can also obtain these numbers from your Chamber of Commerce or fire department.

❑ *Remember, if it cannot fit on the camel, it does not go to the next oasis!* Do you really need it? This is your best opportunity to lighten your load. Do not take to your next home all the things you no longer need from this one. Resist the temptation. If you still feel you must keep that article or box, then do so and label it accordingly.

❑ At the end of the day or the next morning, make a trip to the thrift store. Hire someone with a pickup truck to take the things from your driveway that must go to the landfill.

❑ Finally relax! Treat yourself and your helpers — go out for dinner. When you come home, soak in a soothing bubble bath with your cup of green tea. Well done!

Clearing your garage of clutter will also help clear your mind and make you feel better physically. Your neighbors will notice and envy your dedication, and if you decide to tell them about your pending move, they may even send your real estate agent one of their friends who wants to move into the neighborhood. You never know where your buyer will come from!

Simple Ways to Feng Shui Your Garage

Feng shui will only be truly effective in an uncluttered space. An area where clutter collects and the energy stagnates does not allow a free and open movement of beneficial and healthy chi. A garage space can often fall under this description, but there are simple ways to improve the flow of energy.

Feng Shui Finishing Touches for the Garage

❑ Clean and repair all doors, including the main door and those that lead to the house and/or yard. These doors get a lot of use and abuse, so consider giving them a fresh coat of paint. If it is especially dreary, the whole garage may need paint. Remove all cobwebs, fingerprints, and stains.

❑ Put larger bulbs in dimly lit areas and especially over a workbench. (Be careful not to exceed the manufacturer's directions for maximum wattage.)

❑ Keep a window open for fresh air that prevents the collection of unhealthy and noxious fumes.

❑ Daily, put a good dose of absorbent material, such as kitty litter, on the oil or grease stains. This will usually remove or minimize those unsightly stains within a week (Repeat as needed). Some detergent and a good scrub brush will do the rest.

❑ Remove filled rubbish bins. While selling your home, take your trash out more frequently and store refuse bins along the side of the house or behind a gate or a fence where they will be out of sight.

❑ Ensure that knobs, handles, and keys work properly and are not loose or sticky. Check to see that door hinges do not squeak.

❑ Check that your main garage door is in good condition and operates safely and easily. Heavy or difficult doors that require extra effort to lift are not good selling points. Some older garage door springs are dangerous and can become like a guided missile if they snap and break under extreme tension. If your springs are exceptionally worn, they are probably unsafe, and it would be money well spent to replace them.

As a brief addendum to our section on the garage, buyers will also inspect any storage area or shed on the property. Storage sheds are great for protecting garden tools, planting accessories, potting soil, or lawn mowers; they can also benefit from simple feng shui treatment. Whatever size your shed may be, make it safe and pleasant to view by removing cobwebs and spiders, clearing out and downsizing your tool collection, and cleaning it thoroughly.

Make Decks, Porches, and Patios Irresistible

At home, we spend some of our most peaceful and enjoyable time outdoors on a porch, patio, or deck. Our spirit is far more serene when we experience the beauty of nature in a tranquil outdoor setting. When assessing your exterior space, remember that feng shui encourages lush plant life, clear moving water, and gentle breezes. In addition to the ambience you create inside your dwelling, you also want to encourage your buyers to linger and savor the outside living spaces of your property.

No matter how small or simple, decks and patios can be made alluring and special. A quiet seating area, a tranquil fountain, colorful flowers and greenery in pots all help to create a natural, inviting retreat energetically removed from the bustle of the outside world. *It is not difficult; so do not miss the opportunity to transform your exterior space into something extraordinary.* Look to see where you have an available electric exterior outlet and determine if it is an appropriate spot for an outside fountain. A patio umbrella for shade is practical and a very inviting design element.

When combined with a circular patio table and chairs, an area such as this beckons to a buyer who may be exhausted from a day of house hunting. Sometimes an anxious buyer doesn't want to wait to get back to the office to write an offer to buy a house — they want to do it on the spot, and a smart agent will gladly accommodate them. Where better to do the paperwork than at an inviting table in a lovely backyard setting? Over the years I have written up several offers to purchase using just such an irresistible patio table!

Checklist for Decks, Patios, and Exterior Areas

❑ Sweep and hose down all deck and patio surfaces, getting into all the corners and crevices. Clean all hand railings thoroughly; tighten any that may be loose.

❑ Wipe down tables, chairs, and benches with soapy water and a stiff brush or cloth and then rinse well. It is a very good sign if a buyer decides to sit down outside and relax awhile!

❑ Place colorful round pots of blooming flowers in odd number groupings where corners of decks or patios have sharp edges or points. Keep these planters well watered. Remove dead blooms. Replace dying flowers with fresh ones as needed.

❑ If possible, find a place on a deck or rear patio for a fountain. Since most of our homes have squared off corners and angular lines, balance these *yang* qualities with a fountain in a rounded *yin* design. Several levels of cascading water are especially attractive. Keep the fountain clean and make sure the direction of the water is moving toward the house to keep feng shui abundance coming in your direction!

❑ If part of the patio roof is covered with older, wavy fiberglass, be sure it is thoroughly cleaned using a power nozzle or stiff broom. Looking up through old leaves and debris is not energetically pleasant; it gives the impression there is trash overhead.

❑ Be sure that wooden patio steps and outside stairs of any kind are sturdy and safe. Occasionally, an older friend or parent will accompany the buyers, and it is important that safety is a primary concern.

❑ Baby proof your setting as much as possible. Real estate agents encourage their buyers to make babysitting arrangements for their younger children since it is very difficult for parents to focus on the home while supervising little ones. Nevertheless, sometimes children are present for house showings.

You Will Fall in Love with Your Property All Over Again!

The only danger in using feng shui techniques to prepare your home for sale is that after doing everything recommended, you may not want to leave. It is normal to fully savor and appreciate the new delightful space you have created. You may have feelings of nostalgia and want to stay. However, keep your focus on your new house and understand this current dwelling and its land have served you well. Now your home is a valuable commodity that you are preparing for someone else to purchase and enjoy.

All's Well That Ends Well

If you have followed even some of the above suggestions, your home, no matter how humble or modest, will be ready to sell. Buyers will no doubt have looked at many properties before making their final decision. *As long as the price for your home is appropriate for the*

neighborhood, what you are offering will stand out as an excellent value. Keep your intention of finding the right buyer for your house clear and focused. Continually and actively visualize yourself moving out of this property and into your next home. Imagine a successful and efficient escrow process and *know* you are well on your way!

Section III

TOOLS OF THE TRADE...

Increase Your
Real Estate Expertise

...from Indian Wisdom

A small minded man weighs
what can hinder him,
and fearful, dares not
set to work.

Difficulties cause the
average man
to leave off what he has begun.

A truly great man
does not slacken
in carrying out
what he has begun,
though obstacles tower
one thousand fold,
until he has succeeded.

8

Show Your Home Skillfully

"The real voyage of discovery lies not in seeking new landscapes, but in having new eyes."

— Marcel Proust

Marlene grew nervous as she looked at the clock again. A real estate agent was bringing a buyer over in a few minutes, and she was anxious about the house looking its best. She had already double-checked everything, but worried they would miss some of her favorite points about the house. The laundry room had just been repainted, custom draperies were hung in the master bedroom, and a new reverse-osmosis unit was installed under the sink. She knew they would also probably miss the corner turntable in the kitchen that was so handy for pots and pans.

Marlene thought about writing a note mentioning these things, then remembered that Donna, her listing agent, had put an amenities list on the back of the information flyer. But what if the buyer did not read it? Although Donna had explained that the showing agent would use the real estate lockbox and that she should leave before they arrived, Marlene just knew it would be better if she stayed. Then she could point out everything the agent was not aware of. Besides, she would like to hear the comments as they went through the house.

The doorbell rang and Marlene opened the door for the prospective buyers and their agent. The buyers seemed like such a nice couple, but they looked so young. How could they possibly afford her home? Since she knew everything they needed to see, Marlene decided to show the clients through the house herself, making sure she left nothing out, and the agent followed along. As they all reached the back door, the young man told his wife that they had seen enough and were ready to go. The home was nice, but just not suitable for them. They thanked Marlene and left.

As she sat at the kitchen table with her cup of tea, Marlene wished they had taken more time to really appreciate the house. She didn't have a chance to point out the expensive planter she had decided to leave behind or the Jacuzzi tub in the master bath. But then, this couple probably couldn't afford the house anyway.

Smart Sellers Listen

When you know an agent is bringing a client to view your home, set the stage and then leave. Even though listing agents usually instruct homeowners to be absent when a buyer is coming, sometimes sellers still insist on personally taking prospective purchasers through the house. By doing this, they risk sabotaging an otherwise great showing of their property. An experienced agent will be gracious and thank the owner for the escort. However, the agent may think: "You are not doing yourself a favor by accompanying us. Instead, you are making the buyer nervous. Please go outside. If there are questions, we will come to find you."

The exception to this rule is when the home is very complex and has hidden details, such as a wine cellar or special security system that someone who has not seen the house previously might miss. Experienced professionals usually will have taken steps to check with the listing agent regarding anything unusual or special about the property before bringing clients. Rarely will the seller need to accompany the prospective buyer and showing agent. If the agent really wants your presence for any reason, he or she will specifically ask you to participate in the tour with the buyers — or at the very least they may request that you be available for help with any questions at the end of the showing.

To be welcomed is one thing, but to be smothered by an overly talkative owner is quite another. ***This inhibits the buyer who wants to be polite but simply cannot relax because the presence of the owner is overpowering.*** To imagine actually living in another person's space, a buyer needs what we will call *energetic freedom* to feel what the home is really all about. The qualities of the house will sink in most effectively when the buyer is not confused by excess stimulation — with the seller nearby, this is all but impossible.

When potential buyers are on their way, put the finishing touches on your home and close the door behind you as you leave to allow the buyer and their agent to be by themselves. Visit a friend, go shopping, or take in a movie — think of this as a reward for a job well done. If children or teenagers must be home during a showing, they should try to be outside or doing something quietly constructive in their rooms. Even this, however, is not the best situation for showing. Instead, if it is appropriate, have them be with friends or a trusted neighbor until the buyers and their agent have left.

Many buyers feel intrusive and do not want to linger in your house if family members are at home. Even if you tell buyers that you do not mind them being there, they will be reluctant to explore the home completely. They will feel they are invading your privacy, and they will not remember as much about your property as they would if they had been able to fully relax and just enjoy the house with their agent.

When an Agent Makes an Appointment

Keep a written list by the telephone of all the agents who call for an appointment. Save their business cards and write the date of the visit on them so that you know who has previewed the property and when. The agent who represents you, called the listing agent, will probably want to contact them for comments about the showing and possible client interest. Getting information back from the agents who showed your property will give you both a good idea of how buyers perceive your home. This feedback is a courtesy that real estate professionals show to each other.

Occasionally, a selling agent who represents the buyer will not leave a business card. This is a bit disconcerting for an owner, because if they made an appointment and have entered your house using the lockbox but not left a card, then you really do not know if they came. With the newer electronic lockbox system used in most areas, your listing agent can check to see whose electronic key has been used to access your house. They can request a computer readout stating exactly which agents have entered using the lockbox and when they were there. Keeping a record of telephone appointments will also be helpful if an agent makes an appointment and then does not come.

Listing agents should be aware of this because it reflects poorly on the manners and courtesy of real estate professionals. Sometimes this happens because an agent simply runs out of time or a buyer decides at the last minute they do not want to see a particular home. Proper real estate etiquette is to *always* re-contact the seller and politely cancel the appointment. This should not be difficult, especially today when most agents have cellular telephones.

If You Are Asked Questions During a Showing

Sometimes the buyers or the agent will have questions while they are viewing your home. If you are present during a showing, it is natural for them to ask you some questions. When this happens, you want to be helpful and at the same time you may feel as though you are being put on the spot. (Yet another good reason for you to be absent during all showings.) **Do not volunteer more information than is necessary.** Also, try not to expand your answers with details. Simply answer the question and then stop speaking. Smile, relax, and be pleasant. Remember, if buyers have questions, they are probably interested. If not, they would have already thanked you and returned to the car.

Homeowners who have direct communication with potential buyers or their agents often experience pitfalls. Sellers should not convey desperation or personal anxiety of any kind regarding the sale.

Discussing the loss of a job, a divorce, or alluding to a recent death of a spouse could weaken your bargaining position or indicate emotional distress. *Inadvertently saying too much simply is not in your best interest.*

Some negotiating leverage could be lost if your situation is perceived to be a fire sale. Whatever has motivated your decision to sell is your business only and need not be shared with anyone other than your listing agent. Try to remain at arm's length with buyers and their representatives. Beyond the information that must be listed on your Seller's Disclosure Statement (explained in Chapter 10), do not give any indication of personal circumstances regarding your sale.

Dealing with a Death or a Divorce while Selling a Home

If there has been a recent divorce or the death of a partner, preventing this *grief energy* from spilling over and affecting the feelings of a buyer is a challenge. In feng shui this is called negative precursor energy. Experienced real estate agents can usually sense if the owner of a home has undergone this kind of a separation because it shows up in obvious ways — half-empty closets, one or more bedrooms devoid of all furnishings, or marks on the wall where pictures have recently been removed. Usually poor housekeeping also reflects the stress in the life of the remaining owner, and there can be a subtle but pervading feeling of sadness or energetic emptiness.

Though we may all experience these tragedies at various times in our life, it is especially challenging, though necessary, to put up a good front when your home is being shown to strangers. If you are in this situation and having a difficult time, ease the burden by asking a good friend, relative, or someone from your church to help you get (and keep) your house presentable during this transition. If possible, consider waiting at least a few months before putting your home on the market in order to give yourself time to emotionally heal and get prepared for the physical transition ahead.

Remember that buyers want a *feel good home* and may shy away from a property that is excessively laden with sadness and grief. They may pass over your house even if it is an excellent buy because the negative energy is so powerful. Taking care of business despite your grieving is easier said than done, but if you do, you will soon have a new home that doesn't carry the difficult emotions and the sad memories.

Another aspect of business in this regard is that you do not want to be taken advantage of by a shrewd buyer who might be a hard negotiator and knows you are going through a difficult emotional time. Here, the advice of an experienced listing agent will be invaluable and help buffer you from this potential treatment during the purchase contract and escrow phases of the sale. Obviously, as a seller, it is not wise to allow information of a divorce or a death to undermine your negotiating position.

Feng Shui and Real Estate Savvy — a Winning Combination

When preparing the house for showing, the whole idea is to encourage buyers to feel comfortable and savor the house as if they are enjoying a fine meal. You want them to stay as long as possible to appreciate all that your home has to offer. If potential buyers stay a long time viewing your property, this is usually an excellent indicator of their level of interest.

Showing agents smile inwardly and silently congratulate the seller who has done their preparation work well. There is little to add about a home that already says it all and says it well. We know that the home that sells itself will not be on the market long. Usually, the most agents have to do is remind buyers this is a good buy and they should consider this property seriously, without much delay, before it is snapped up by another buyer.

After you have prepared your home, think of each buyer viewing your property as if it were opening night of a stage play and you are the director. *Even after numerous showings, do not get complacent about keeping your stage set.* Keep your own enthusiasm up and the performance fresh knowing your goal is in sight. Many of the following feng shui suggestions will seem familiar. They are techniques that have proven successful over time. Much of what feng shui teaches is basic common sense — and after four thousand years, it still works!

Feng Shui Showing Checklist

❑ **Check your mouth of chi:** Be certain the entire entry area is swept clean and is welcoming. Fresh flowers are especially recommended for this area. If the weather is dark or stormy, turn on your porch light.

❑ **Encourage serenity:** Play soft background music. Turn the television *off*. If a showing takes place when children are home, caution them not to play video games or loud music.

❑ **Unblock interior chi:** Reposition any furniture obstructing pathways.

❑ **Keep safety and comfort foremost:** Make sure rugs are not curled along an edge or positioned so as to cause an accident. Use non-slip lining under area carpets that have even the slightest tendency to move. You want your buyer to fall *for* your house, not *in* it!

❑ **Activate welcoming energy:** Have a fire burning in the fireplace, especially on a cold or dark day. Turn on non-glare lights where appropriate.

❑ **Arouse the senses**: Yes! Bake banana bread or chocolate chip cookies before a showing. Leave some for the buyer and sales agent! Aromatherapy works too — Jami Lin highly recommends pine, cinnamon, and tangerine scents to make a home warm and inviting.

❑ **Encourage physical comfort:** Check the temperature and keep the thermostat around 65-70 degrees. Since even subtle background noises are distracting, try to avoid the sound of whirring fans or air conditioners.

❑ **Let the beauty of nature come in:** Open the shades and raise the blinds. Open several windows for ventilation.

❑ **Check that chi is not draining away:** Put toilet lids down. Close shower doors and curtains. Close bathroom doors or leave them only slightly ajar.

❑ **Remove distracting elements:** Take barking dogs for a walk or a ride in the car. *Even if your dog does not bark, you are well advised to take him elsewhere.* Other noisy items such as washing machines, dryers, and dishwashers are best turned off during showings.

❑ **Protect your privacy:** Turn off the volume on your answering machine so incoming messages from friends or family will not be heard while potential buyers are in the house.

❑ **Use common sense:** Put away any jewelry or valuables of any kind. Real estate agents do their best to screen their clients and to stay with them at all times during a showing, but, unfortunately, this is not always possible.

❑ **Clear your clutter:** Before leaving, take a walk through the house. Make sure the beds are made, the dirty clothes are in hampers, and the toys are in bins. If dishes are in the sink, put an attractive dishtowel over them or place everything in the dishwasher. If your office is at home, clear your desktop or at least stack papers neatly.

9

Smart Sellers Hire Professionals

"To be conscious that you lack awareness is a great step to knowledge."

— Benjamin Disraeli

Patti and Jack have been thinking about whether they should list their home with a real estate agent or save the commission and put that money toward their new purchase. They want to move to the country, buy some acreage, and build their dream house. To do this, they feel they are going to need every penny from the sale of their current property. Jack has a pretty good idea of the general value of their place, and has figured that a six percent commission on their house will come to over $15,000. This money could be part of the down payment on the land they want to find.

Several months ago, their neighbors Mike and Christi tried to sell their house without a real estate agent and had a terrible experience. They trusted their buyer when he told them he qualified for the bank loan, but just before escrow was to close, his supposed "gift" down payment never materialized. They bitterly regretted the lost months of marketing the house and waiting for this buyer to perform. Finally, after such a discouraging and costly experience, Mike and Christi listed their house, agreed to pay the commission, and quickly sold their house to a qualified buyer.

Since both Patti and Jack worked in sales and had financial knowledge, they thought they knew how to market their property. They felt they could show their home well, and that it wouldn't be too hard to assess a buyer's credit worthiness. Although Patti was a little nervous about having strangers coming in, Jack made a list of questions to ask to screen out unqualified callers.

Wanting to save the commission money, they finally decided to sell the house themselves while searching for property to buy. Jack made a "For Sale by Owner" sign; they wrote a short ad for the local paper, and decided which days they should advertise. Although the ad cost more than they expected, they felt that if it attracted good buyers it would be worth the price. So, they put up their sign and waited.

In four days Patti and Jack received 12 calls. Most callers wanted their address and insisted on driving by before doing anything more; several wanted to know if their loan was assumable, if the sellers would carry paper, and at what rate and term. One man said he was calling from a pay phone and could only look at the house on his lunch hour, which was when Jack was away each day; that meant Patti would be home by herself. One lady, Penny, was very pleasant on the phone and said that she and her husband, Ken, were visiting from the Midwest where they were trying to sell their farm, and they would like to come over about 6 o'clock.

That evening Penny and Ken were friendly, easy to talk to, and loved the house. Penny had heard about California termites and wanted to know if Patti and Jack would guarantee that the house would be treated for them. Jack didn't know if the house had termites, but he assured them he would take care of those details. After going through the house and yard, they sat around the dining room table and discussed the purchase.

Ken explained that their farm had been for sale for several months, but recently there had been a lot of interest. They were in town for a week and definitely wanted to buy a house. He and Penny really liked this one and felt they would be happy here. Though the price seemed right, they would still need to get a loan for the difference between what they would get from selling their farm and the cost of Patti and Jack's property.

Farming was depressed in their area, but they felt certain a good buyer would turn up shortly. As soon as they sold their land and farm operation, they would be able to close this escrow. Ken said they had $3,000 they could put up as a deposit and would be willing to write a check tonight. Patti and Jack looked at each other and said they needed to talk it over.

What to do? They both really liked these people and wanted them to have a chance to buy their house, but they were worried. How would they keep a close eye on the sale of the farm so far away? Penny and Ken seemed so honest, and hadn't haggled over their price. Their explanation about needing to sell their farm sounded reasonable. If they accepted this proposal, what would they tell other buyers? Should they discourage other people by telling them they had already accepted a deposit? The proceeds from the *farm's sale would provide most of their asking price, but Patti wondered if Penny and Ken would qualify for a loan for the difference.*

Patti and Jack weren't comfortable with the arrangement, but they decided they could give Penny and Ken a few months to sell their farm. They filled in the blanks of a form Jack had bought from the local stationery store, and Ken wrote the deposit check. They all shook hands. Penny was excited and asked Patti if she could walk through the house again, while Ken wanted to see the garage one more time. He said they would be driving home the next morning to try to speed up the sale of their farm. After they left, Patti and Jack looked at each other, and then at the signed contract on the table. This was not exactly happening the way they had planned.

Are You a Riverboat Gambler?

The sale of your home will probably take several months and involve hundreds of thousands of dollars. How much are you willing to gamble that you can put all the technical and legal pieces of a transaction together without professional help? The proverbial riverboat gambler knows his game and may make a modest living at it if he is lucky. However, his type continually lives on the edge and has a risk mentality.

You will not find a wise seller wanting to play a game like this. He or she knows the stakes are too high. Sellers are experienced in their own line of work, but know little about the complex legalities of a real estate transaction. Looking at the cards in their hand and giving it careful consideration, smart sellers decide to hire an experienced real estate professional to do all the technical work.

Even if you are an experienced investor who has bought and sold properties for years, I strongly recommend that you not try to sell your own home. Constantly changing legal requirements in the world of real estate require the expertise of a knowledgeable and full-time professional. How can a novice take care of all the governmental requirements, accurately complete the necessary forms, make all the proper disclosures, legally protect both buyer and the seller, and do all of this in a specified time?

You might give the whole process a valiant try, and in the end unhappily discover that it's just not worth the legal and financial risk. In the meantime, you have wasted valuable time, energy, and money trying to step into the shoes of a real estate professional. Selling your home is a major decision and one that you have come to after careful consideration. ***Once that determination has been made, your next thought should be about which real estate agent will do the best job for you.***

At Your Service

An experienced real estate agent can make all the difference in your selling transaction. ***Here are some of the many details an agent will take care of to ensure a successful close of escrow:***

✓ Give expert guidance on appropriate pricing.

✓ Help you decide what your home needs to help it sell faster.

- ✓ Advertise the home in appropriate local (or out of area) magazines and newspapers.

- ✓ Place your property in the local (and/or nearby) multiple listing systems.

- ✓ Provide a professional sign and a box of information flyers.

- ✓ Hold open house showings on weekends.

- ✓ Screen potential buyers to verify they are financially qualified to buy your home.

- ✓ Network with other real estate professionals about the advantages of your property.

- ✓ Help with negotiations on offers regarding price and terms.

- ✓ Act as a knowledgeable trouble-shooter on unusual buyer's requests.

- ✓ Provide useful contacts with necessary inspectors they know to be dependable.

- ✓ Give guidance through difficulties during escrow.

- ✓ Keep track of paperwork and seller requirements in escrow.

- ✓ Make sure the buyer and their lender follow through with financial details.

- ✓ Stay on top of the entire escrow procedure.

- ✓ Give guidance about last minute moving details to transfer your home to the new buyer.

Using the services of a real estate professional will pay you handsome rewards. A good agent can make a difficult sale smoother and successfully sell what might otherwise be a very unmarketable property. They will see problems before they arise and take care of them before they become impossible. ***They will sell your house!***

Selecting Your Agent —
Take Time, Choose Wisely

As a seller, selecting a real estate agent is one of the most important decisions you will make. To find a quality agent who will represent your interests, talk to friends and neighbors who have recently sold their homes. Also visit or call several local title or escrow companies who work with agents on a daily basis.

Ask for recommendations about which salespersons:

✓ Have years of experience

✓ Close (not just open) the most escrows

✓ Work well with all types of people

✓ Listen carefully

✓ Are highly respected by their peers

You will want to get a list of these full-time professionals and then arrange to interview each of them. If an agent is working part-time at another job, they may not be available if an offer or a counter-offer needs to be presented immediately; their client in this case is the loser. In the business of real estate, *time is of the essence,* and an effective agent needs to be AVAILABLE.

The agent with the most listings advertised in the newspaper is not necessarily the one who will devote the most time to selling your home. Agents with lots of listings tend to spread themselves thinly. They are not only representing you, they have oodles of sellers. They often have full-time assistants, which certainly helps. However, the personal touch, including frequent telephone contact, is sometimes lacking. It is nearly impossible to adequately market dozens of properties while still treating each seller in a special, individual way.

Every agent has his or her own style of getting the job done. A major portion of time needs to be spent keeping in close contact with a seller as the listing moves forward. Often, an agent who has fewer listings can give a seller much more individualized attention and produce greater, and possibly faster, results. You will want to select a full-time agent who has plenty of experience, but be aware that experience alone does not necessarily ensure a good choice.

The Best Real Estate Listing Agent Will:

✓ *Listen carefully...* and read between the lines for your needs about the sale. They need to be almost intuitive about subtleties that will be important to you throughout the transaction (such as how much time you might need to get organized and be ready to move).

✓ *Explain details thoroughly...* and give good advice about the correct asking price for your property. They will explain and show you what you need to do to get your asking price. It is important that you feel comfortable asking your agent to explain real estate terminology, and any contract or negotiating details you don't understand. When the time comes, rapport and clear communication can make the vital difference in how much profit you retain at the end of the sale.

✓ *Be a fount of local knowledge…* and fully up to date on current market conditions and comparative sales in your area. They should know which properties similar to yours have sold recently and if there were any unusual circumstances with those transactions which may have affected the selling price, such as a death, bankruptcy, or divorce. They should be able to explain why a particular house sold in your neighborhood, such as quality remodeling, recent re-roofing or painting, and what you can do to increase the chances that yours will sell quickly.

✓ *Be a good and frequent communicator…* and contact you several times each week. You will want them to check in with you regarding agents who have shown your property and follow up with helpful feedback.

✓ *Be flexible and allow you flexibility too…* and give you plenty of information about which properties are selling so you will understand what price you will be able to get for your home. They will encourage you to respond to, but not necessarily take, each offer submitted, pointing out the strengths and weaknesses of each, eventually helping you decide which offer is the right one. [16]

Now that you know what to look for in a listing agent, you will be better equipped to make a wise selection. This process does take a bit of extra time, but you'll end up a happier (and more profitable!) seller because you have based your choice on solid reasoning. When you have at least three or four names of top agents who have been highly recommended to you, contact them and explain that you are in the process of selecting a listing agent to help sell your home. Then…

---

[16] "Look Beyond Experience for Agent," by Llyce R. Glink, *Los Angeles Times,* Real Estate Section, April 23, 2000.

Set up a meeting with them individually at your property and request that each agent bring:

✓ Examples of advertising they and their office do on a regular basis. This can include monthly newsletters, newspaper, and magazine ads, or any other method they use to attract buyers. Internet marketing is an important tool today. They should be able to access their website to show you how your home will appear on the web.

✓ Information about themselves and their office, giving background, size, and how long they have been in business. Well-established firms usually command a good degree of community respect. However a newer office may be highly motivated to *move your listing.* If the company is only recently in business, it is a good idea to get their promises of advertising in writing.

✓ A competitive market analysis (CMA) showing what price would be most appropriate for your home in the current market, based on similar sales in your neighborhood in the past six months. *They should leave this with you for further study.*

✓ Names and telephone numbers of several recent sellers they have helped so you can request a personal recommendation.

Interviewing Prospective Listing Agents

Spend at least an hour or two with each prospective listing agent. Ask about their background, experience, and methods for selling properties. Allow adequate time to do a complete tour of your home and yard.

Checklist of Questions to Ask Potential Listing Agents

❑ Do they sell real estate full-time?

❑ How many years of experience do they have?

❑ Do they belong to the National Association of REALTORS®?

❑ What is their commission; how much goes to the selling office?

❑ Are all of their listings placed in the Multiple Listing Service?

❑ Are all of their office's listings on the Internet?

❑ Do they hold open houses? How frequently?

❑ How do they feel your house should be made available for showing? By lockbox or by appointment? In larger areas, which multiple-listing databases do they subscribe to?

❑ Do they advertise all of their listings at the same time in local newspapers and real estate magazines? (Some offices rotate the advertising of listings.)

❑ How often will they keep in touch with you during the listing?

Before they leave, be sure to have them make a list of at least five things they feel you should do to sell your home faster. Ask them to put this in writing or take careful notes on their suggestions as you walk through your home, garage, and yard together. Allow adequate time for this process, remembering they are seeing your property for the first time. Keep a file or notebook where you record your written impressions. Pay special attention to each agent's personality and how comfortable you feel communicating with them. Tune in to their sincerity, integrity, knowledge, and personal style.

Every Home Sale is Part of a Larger Picture

Every real estate sale is unique. Though they share similarities, each transaction is special and different from every other. *Selling homes is about people, not just property,* and it can be a highly emotional time for you and your family. Perhaps you are moving out of state and need to coordinate a purchase across the country. Maybe you are getting married and trying to sell one house, buy another, and relocate near a good school. You might be struggling with a divorce and dealing with many intense issues as well as selling a home. You may be elderly or have recently lost a mate and need extra attention and guidance.

An agent must understand what you are trying to achieve and comprehend the whole picture. Since each case will be different, they should give you their undivided attention as you explain your personal situation and needs. Being efficient is important, but if their manner and method of selling real estate is all business with no personal touch or understanding, you will feel frustrated and as if you are just another one of many files in their drawer of listings.

In these days of high technology, you may be visited by an agent with a laptop computer that instantly brings up a market analysis of your home's value. Some agents will print out elaborate flyers as you sit at your dining room table. They may have fancy web sites and digital cameras to display your home in an impressive ad. All of this is great, but don't get carried away with the *tech* and forget the *personal touch.* It is especially important that you and your agent have clear and open communication, or you may end up resentful and unhappy. If you feel intimidated or cannot adequately communicate with one person, move on to the next candidate.

After you have interviewed each agent, ***make the telephone calls to speak with their recent sellers***. This is time well spent, so take the hour or so to hear first-hand how they performed in previous transactions. Remember that you are entrusting this person with, very probably, the most expensive object you have ever owned, and you will be working together closely through close of escrow. *Choose wisely.*

When you finally select an agent, listen to them. If you did not already ask your listing agent to make a list of the things that would most help get your home sold, now is the time. Go slowly and thoroughly through your home together and ask your agent to be brutally honest about what could help sell the house faster. ***You want specific suggestions about what to remove, clean up, and repair.*** Take care of these things **BEFORE** the property officially goes on the market and the "For Sale" sign goes up.

How the Real Estate Commission Works

Some of the most common misconceptions and misunderstandings among the general public are about real estate commissions, how they are divided, and who gets what. The amount of commission is usually based on a percentage of the selling price of the property. The escrow officer will verify this amount with the seller early in the escrow and again before releasing a check to the broker when the transaction is recorded in the new buyer's name.

When first discussing listing your property, you and the agent you have selected will negotiate this sales fee (the commission) and you will be shown the exact dollar amount that will be deducted from your proceeds. The agent should give you a Seller's Net Cost Sheet with all fees clearly written down. This cost of the commission will vary from the initial quote only if the final, agreed-upon purchase price is different from the original listing price. If the sales price does change, simply multiply the final agreed-upon sales price by the agreed-upon percentage for the commission. (For example: $300,000 x 6% = $18,000.)

Your listing agent will receive only a percentage of the listing commission. A sizeable portion of the commission goes to the broker's office, which bears full professional responsibility, contractual accountability, and legal liability for each transaction. This is not only normal business practice, but also real estate common sense. The broker of record is the person whom the State Department of Real Estate holds liable in the event of malpractice or any unlawful conduct in the practice of business.

If a lawsuit is filed, it is the *broker* who is named in the legal proceedings. It is significant to understand that the broker (not your agent) is taking all the risks, as well as receiving the financial compensation. Since the broker is where the buck stops, they are paid for this accountability according to a prior agreed-upon commission split with his or her agents.

When an agent from a different real estate office brings you the buyer, the office representing the buyer becomes the selling agent, and the original total commission will then be shared with that office's broker at close of escrow. Your listing agent's office will receive whatever portion you agreed to and the brokerage representing the buyer will usually receive half of the total commission on the listing contract you signed.

For example:
Listing price of the property is $350,000
Real estate commission is 6%
$350,000 x .06 = $21,000   total commission

Listing Broker (represents the seller) .03 = $10,500 1/2 total commission
Selling Broker (represents the buyer) .03 = $10,500 1/2 total commission

Although it is customary for the seller to pay the real estate commission, sometimes buyers will employ and pay for their own buyer's broker. In that case, as a seller you will not pay the commission to the buyer's agent. The buyer takes care of that through a contract with their broker. *However, in most transactions the total commission is paid by the seller directly to the listing brokerage office (not to your listing agent), and is taken out of the seller's proceeds at the close of escrow.*

There are variations on this, and because commissions are negotiable, you can arrange with your broker to pay a flat fee, a lesser amount, or whatever percentage the two of you agree on. The office that brings you the buyer will be given the percentage printed in the Multiple Listing Service (MLS) database information, which is based on your listing agreement. The percentage amount published in the multiple listing book is contractual. In other words, you have already agreed to pay this percentage to the office that brings your buyer. Ask your listing agent to explain this further.

Your listing agent will prepare a "Seller's Net Proceeds" form mentioned earlier, which lists all your charges in the selling process. These include title fees, escrow costs, real estate commission, homeowners' association transfer fee (if any), recording costs, and other miscellaneous charges in connection with paying off your old loan. This form will show you how much money you will have at close of escrow. This is called the *equity* in your property. Equity is the amount you receive for your property minus what you owe. Your agent or the escrow officer during the escrow process should thoroughly explain what all the various costs represent. (Refer to *The Life of an Escrow* in Appendix F.) Be sure to ask your agent questions and get answers that make sense and satisfy you.

By Law, Real Estate Commissions are Negotiable!

Price-fixing of real estate commissions is illegal. This legislation goes back to the era of the Sherman Anti-Trust laws, and prohibits fixed commissions on both national and local levels. California and a number of other states now print "**real estate commissions are negotiable**" in boldface type on the listing agreement contract. Fixing of commissions is further prohibited by the **National Association of REALTORS®** Code of Ethics. Because you only want to be represented by professionals who adhere to this important professional code and standard of doing business, be sure to verify that your agent, and his or her brokerage office, are members in good standing with this national professional trade association.

You and your listing agent should discuss the commission and define the amount you will pay at the beginning of your meeting. **If a real estate agent or broker insists that a fixed commission is the only way to do business, get another agent.**

Showing Your Home by Lockbox or by Appointment

Years ago, a fairly unsophisticated lockbox worked with a simple three-digit combination, similar to the one you used on your high school gym locker. The key to your home was inside. This system worked fairly well, but the problem was keeping the combination secure. Today in most areas, each agent pays for an electronic key device that is computer coded with his or her name and brokerage office. The code for entry is changed monthly, and an agent's entry capability can be electronically denied for professional reasons or restricted to certain hours of the day. An example of this lockbox restriction to an agent might be as simple as not having paid their professional dues, or as serious as being investigated by the Department of Real Estate for a business code violation.

The newer lockbox system works quite well. The box itself can hang from a doorknob, a water spigot pipe, a gate, or any strong, immovable object. Your listing agent will help select the best place so agents won't have to hunt for it and waste time while their buyers are waiting.

Using a lockbox to gain access to your property allows agents the freedom to show your home when you are unavailable to let them in. The process is simple. An agent will first call your telephone number, listed in the MLS (Multiple Listing Service) book, to make an appointment. If you are not home and their client is ready to see your property, the agent leaves you a message (yes, you do need a message machine or voice mail of some kind), saying when they will be coming to look at your house. If you are still not home when they arrive, the lockbox is used. *The lockbox allows you to go about your daily life without missing a potential buyer.*

Having your home shown only by appointment can be restrictive for agents with a large number of properties to show on any given day. Sometimes a client is only in town for a few hours or over a weekend, and you may not be available. Your listing agent might be with other clients and unable to meet prospective buyers at your property at a convenient time. Usually agents will take their clients to the homes that are the easiest to show. If your listing requires an appointment, it may be skipped over because arranging a showing time on short notice may be inconvenient. Putting the buyer's agent in that position is not to your benefit.

Exceptions to this appointment scenario are the very high-priced listings that require special financial qualifications for purchase. Buyers for homes in this rarified price category usually have to schedule appointments for homes they want to look at with the listing agent, who will take them through. For most homes, however, keep it simple and make showing your property as hassle-free as possible.

The Length of a Listing

Most listings are taken for three to six months. This is flexible, and you can list your property for a shorter period in a hot market to give your agent greater incentive to make the sale. However, try not to be difficult. There is some lag time between the date you sign the listing and when it actually appears in the MLS database, in newspapers, and in glossy real estate magazines. Listing your property for less than three months is too limiting. You need to give your agent time to get your advertising done well and then manage the resulting calls. Do not be unreasonable and put your agent under impossible deadlines, which will only add stress and alienate him or her. If you are happy with your listing agent, the advertising they have done, the communication they have maintained with you, and the showings that have come as a result of their efforts, you have the option of extending your listing.

Caution: **It is in your best interest to keep your home consistently in the MLS database and in front of the buying public.** Jumping from office to office is a hint to other agents that you might be difficult or stubborn to work with. Noting that you have had your home listed with several different offices, agents may decide to avoid a problem seller and direct their clients to other properties. This is another reason to spend quality time choosing an excellent brokerage office to represent you right from the start.

Careful Buyers and Sellers Are Professionally Represented

Remember, the vast majority of homebuyers are represented by a real estate agent. You will encounter real estate professionals from the buyer's side; it is prudent that you also be represented by a skilled professional. If you try to be your own advocate, you will be at a distinct disadvantage; the buyer will have a knowledgeable champion in his corner knowing and negotiating all the legal details. You will be technically outweighed and probably outsmarted.

Your agent will handle the showing and scheduling of the broker caravan (when all the agents in the multiple listing system are able to come through your home on a designated day). Your agent will advertise in the paper and in real estate magazines, and prepare and print flyers for people driving by your house. In other words, you can relax, knowing you have a champion in your corner.

When offers start coming in and buyers' agents are applying pressure — the tension will build. You will be so relieved to have an experienced agent on your side, advising and negotiating in your behalf. They will help you secure the highest price for your property and save you considerable headaches, stress, and in the long run, money!

10

Mastering Full Disclosure

"...This above all, to thine own self be true; and it must follow, as the night the day, thou canst not then be false to any man..."

— "Hamlet," William Shakespeare

John and Marsha are getting ready to sell their house. Although they have enjoyed living in this property for the past four years, they remember that when they bought the house the previous owners had not told them about the drainage problem in the back yard. Soon after John and Marsha moved in, heavy rains washed away a good part of their large lower flowerbed, which ended up in their neighbor's side yard. Their neighbor told them this soil slippage had been a problem for several years and had been a real nuisance. Hadn't the former owners mentioned it?

John and Marsha went to their purchase file and checked over the seller's real estate transfer disclosure statement; however, nothing referred to any drainage problem or erosion. After several rainstorms and more topsoil lost down the embankment, they ended up paying a licensed contractor $3,000 to install a retaining wall that would prevent further erosion. Their real estate agent at the time suggested they go back and question the previous owner and listing broker. Though disappointed and upset, John and Marsha did not want to stir up trouble after so many months had gone by.

Now John and Marsha are the sellers, and when Mike, their current real estate agent, met with them to take their listing, he presented them with the required disclosure documentation. They discussed existing problems regarding the house, the lot in general, and also any problems affecting the property that had already been corrected. Recalling how badly they felt over the drainage problem not being disclosed to them, John and Marsha then shared their story about the erosion in the back yard. Mike wrote everything down, noting that the problem had been fixed.

Mike went through the entire disclosure form with them and explained that in California, and numerous other states, this step is considered so important that it carries a three day right of rescission for the buyer. If any disclosed fact is so serious that the buyer does not wish to proceed, he or she may cancel the transaction. The seller must be painstakingly thorough and accurate with disclosure, since many lawsuits result from an owner who has knowingly withheld important information.

Mike told them that they probably could have taken the previous owners to small claims court because there was evidence they knowingly had not disclosed the drainage problem. He gave them examples of court cases in which sellers were sued for this lack of disclosure. Mike's real estate company prides itself on satisfied clients, and he praised John and Marsha for being so thorough on their disclosure form.

He cautioned that it is important to reveal and deal with any problems early in the selling process. If a buyer is going to back out because of a problem with the house, it is far better that it happen sooner rather than after weeks or months of escrow. This way, sellers will not have turned away other potential buyers who might have been able to live with the difficulty.

Eyes Wide Shut

This is the Age of Real Estate Disclosure. Sellers of property are under the legal requirement to disclose, disclose, and disclose. Smart sellers will hire a real estate professional who will give them a detailed form for disclosing all material facts or problems. Even if you decide to try to sell your home without experienced representation, you still must fully disclose!

As far as feng shui and disclosure are concerned, balance and harmony are always the goals. *On an energetic level, we attract back to us what we send out to others* In other words, it goes back to the old adage, "what goes around, comes around." If you are not honest and forthright about explaining problems regarding your house, you put the integrity of the transaction out of balance.

As a result, one day you too may be the victim of a dishonest seller. By failing to divulge a material problem about a property, you seriously tempt legal fate as well as inviting bad karma. Neighbors are very observant, and the plumbing repair truck constantly parked in your driveway is a sure tip-off that something has been amiss. The neighbors will probably mention this to your new buyers. If you fail to disclose your plumbing history (or any other problem), you risk severe buyer's remorse and possibly an expensive lawsuit.

Buyers usually realize that every home, even a brand new one, will have a few problems. They know that some difficulties are larger and more serious than others and that even the most elegant dwelling will have a few warts. Structural dilemmas do not just simply disappear or have some sort of spontaneous remission; instead, like mushrooms, they grow in the dark!

A leaky roof, inadequate water drainage, soil slippage, and poor electrical circuitry (among other serious problems) can come back to haunt you months and even years after a sale. Imagine the property damage and perhaps human loss that, for example, an electrical fire could cause. If safety items have not already been taken care of for your own well being as an occupant, prepare to get them corrected now. Of course, always use *licensed* contractors when making repairs.

Moisture problems are in a class all by themselves. Water can cause serious and often hidden damage that, over time, ruins wood floors, areas under sinks and around toilets, showers, and tubs. These places, in particular, harbor dry rot, which a thorough home and termite inspection will usually uncover.

Mildew and related odors are also not always immediately noticeable and may only be detected after the buyer moves in. You can be sure, however, that the buyer and his or her attorney will establish the fact that you, the seller, must have been aware of such a condition, having lived in the house for so long. If items such as these have not been revealed, prepare yourself for a nasty, threatening letter and all the ensuing headaches. All this could have been avoided had the condition been disclosed.

Permits or No Permits —
That Is the Question

Any room addition or structural modification in a house should have been made with an appropriate city building permit. A permit usually entails a city building inspector's approval as each phase of the project is completed to insure that building codes have been followed. However, permits are not always obtained when remodeling work is done; ***if there is no permit for any structural modification in your home, this needs to be disclosed***. This is a common though usually not insurmountable problem. Sometimes a buyer will accept the property modification *as is*, without a permit. However, insurance companies may not compensate an owner if a fire occurs and no permit for the damaged area exists.

If the buyer insists a permit be obtained, you may be required to pay a nominal fine for the city building department to inspect the work and issue a permit. Try not to turn this into a drama; rather do what is necessary and get on with the transaction. Usually your real estate agent can be a valuable asset in a case like this and may be able to do some of the time consuming legwork for you. Try not to let something relatively small become a *deal breaker.* You will no doubt have the same issue with any other serious buyer, so you might as well keep this buyer and get the escrow closed.

Selling *As Is* — or What Lies Beneath?

When a property is sold *as is* the seller is offering the property for sale, and letting the buyer know up front they are not going to fix all the items on a possible buyer's request list. In other words, what the buyer sees is what the buyer gets. Buyers understand an older home cannot be rebuilt to be new again, and at the same time, buying *as is* puts a special responsibility on them and their real estate agent to be very cautious. Every time a buyer considers purchasing, it is important to have thorough and adequate inspections of all aspects of a property —especially with an *as is* property.

When a house is being sold *as is*, it tells the buyer there are items needing repair or correcting; this may lower the seller's negotiating advantage somewhat. Before you, the seller, decide to take this course, consider that you may not necessarily be able to ask top dollar for a product in need of repairs. After all, if a buyer purchases a property and then has to spend a considerable sum of money to correct things that the seller was not willing to fix, there will need to be some adjustment in asking price or final negotiated sales amount.

If you intend to market your property *as is*, be clear about it. *This fact needs to be shown in the listing information and made available to real estate agents.* It is not something that you casually mention as an afterthought to prospective purchasers. Discuss all this with your listing agent and ask their advice. If the decision is to proceed, the words *as is* should be in your advertising and on information flyers; otherwise buyers will think that should an item come up during an inspection that they want fixed, that the seller will oblige.

Selling *as is* Still Requires Full Disclosure

Selling a home "as is" does not relieve a seller of his or her responsibility to disclose all material facts and problems about the property. A material fact is anything about the property of a physical or structural nature that might alter a buyer's decision. It is information you would appreciate knowing if you were the buyer. A fully informed buyer then makes the choice whether or not to proceed.

The owner, not the agent, should directly fill out the Seller's Transfer Disclosure form. If the property has been a rental unit, and the seller has not lived in it, the seller should still fill out the form and have the tenant make any further disclosures on a supplemental separate page. The occupant is much more likely to have a better sense of the property and what problems it may have.

After a sales contract has been signed, the buyer should receive the disclosure form immediately. Since disclosure allows the purchaser a three day right of rescission, it would seem in everyone's best interest to have them obtain this information at the earliest possible time. As of this writing, in California, the law requires that disclosure be made ***prior to close of escrow***. However, the California Association of REALTORS® contract stipulates within "five days of acceptance." The main idea here is that the buyer should be given the disclosure information as soon as possible since the contents may influence their decision to purchase.

If a known defect has *not* been discovered during the home inspection, it is poor judgment **not** to inform the buyer of anything serious the owner is aware of. For example, a wise seller will not wait until the eleventh hour to mention that the fireplace chimney has a serious crack. This gives the buyer a legal way to back out of the transaction. In any case you will most likely end up paying for the cost of fixing the fireplace or giving the buyer credit in escrow for the price of the repairs. Take care of these types of problems and disclose all material facts as early as possible.

If they feel they are being treated honestly and fairly, most buyers will work with the seller towards a successful close of escrow. However, if a home inspection turns up major problems that the seller probably knew about and did not disclose, the buyer becomes uneasy and wonders what else he or she has not been told. Distrust quickly surfaces and jeopardizes the sale.

With Disclosure, Nice Guys Finish First

Sellers sometimes hope that by not mentioning a problem to a buyer it will somehow go away or will not be apparent. This is not only faulty logic, but also very bad feng shui! Why take the risk and even lose sleep worrying that the problem, whatever it is, will recur? You know it probably will, and when it does it will come back to hit you behind the knees or squarely in the stomach as the process server hands you the lawsuit papers.

As you and your agent go through your home in detail, take note together of all items needing disclosure. As a real estate professional, he or she is trained to be very thorough. However, *only you* will know of less obvious things. **Approach this process as if YOU were the buyer.** What would you appreciate knowing about this home and property? It is far better to err on the side of caution regarding small items for disclosure such as minor tears in linoleum or chips in tile. By including these less important facts, you will have done your job well, and the buyer will feel confident you are operating from a position of integrity. *This is good feng shui.*

Reminders...
to Get You Started with Disclosure

Some typical disclosure items are included here as examples to start your thinking. *If you have to ask yourself, "Should I reveal this?" the answer is YES.*

❑ Splits or gouges in linoleum, especially under places which are not easily seen (i.e., under refrigerator)

❑ Cracks in counter or floor tiles

❑ Electric sockets that do not work

❑ Torn or damaged carpet under furniture

❑ Appliances that operate inconsistently or need repair

❑ Leaking water heater, sinks, or faucets

❑ Windows painted shut

❑ Leaking windows or skylights

❑ Broken seals in dual-pane windows

❑ Torn or missing window screens

❑ Stains in carpeting that will not come out

If it's broken or needs repair, fix it.

Disclosure Beyond Your Property Line

It is not enough to only disclose material facts about existing problems within your home and parcel of land. *You must also reveal anything you know about adjacent properties or your neighborhood that might affect a buyer's decision.* Here is a partial list to consider:

✓ City or school busses on a regular route past property

✓ School facility with loudspeakers, bells, and increased traffic

- ✓ Stadium lights for evening sporting events
- ✓ Airport or flight path with airplanes operating within hearing distance
- ✓ Noisy neighbors, practicing rock bands, constant teen youth group activity
- ✓ Neighborhood dogs that bark constantly or are allowed to run without leashes
- ✓ Hospital zone with sirens from emergency vehicles
- ✓ Nearby church or meeting hall whose overflow parking impacts your street
- ✓ Noise from heavy equipment operating nearby
- ✓ Upcoming major construction near your property
- ✓ New freeway or on-ramp being proposed
- ✓ Odors from a nearby factory, processing plant, or other facility
- ✓ Pesticides or other air-borne chemicals being used on nearby farms or nurseries
- ✓ Toxic waste dumps, public trash land fills, or oil refineries nearby
- ✓ Any potential zoning change in the nearby area you may have knowledge of

Shine Some Light in Dark Places

Be aware that as a seller you can hire your own home inspector. By having a professional home inspection report ready and waiting for a buyer, you have already de-mystified the house and provided answers to any potential questions — you have gone the extra mile. The buyer will probably have his own professional home inspection made; two independent opinions are fine. The point is that you have exceeded expectations and provided a professional opinion of your home's structural worthiness. Especially if you are selling your property *as is*, this additional step gives buyers the confidence that even though they are buying the home in its present condition, at least they know what that means.

California real estate law makes it very clear that agents have specific responsibilities when it comes to disclosure. "It is the duty of a licensed real estate broker or salesperson… to conduct a reasonably competent and diligent visual inspection of the residential property comprising one to four dwelling units, or a manufactured home, offered for sale and to disclose to that prospective purchaser all facts materially affecting the value or desirability of the property…" [17] Your listing agent will conduct a thorough, visual inspection and make appropriate notations on the Seller's Transfer Disclosure Statement.

No amount of good feng shui advice can make up for dishonesty. Integrity never goes out of style. This is your shining opportunity to be the good guy. Do what you would appreciate others doing to you. Do the right thing and DISCLOSE! Your buyer will appreciate your honesty, and so will you.

---

[17] California Civil Code; Section 2079 – 2079.5

A Home Warranty Policy — a Wise Choice

A home warranty insures coverage of most physical aspects of a house for one year from close of escrow. Today, most offers to purchase include the buyer's request that a seller provide this coverage in the event something becomes inoperative after the sale. Many companies provide excellent protection, each with slightly different aspects, but for the most part they are relatively similar.

Often a listing agent will encourage a seller to include this home warranty protection up front with the sale. This is an excellent idea, and some warranty programs include seller's coverage that protects the seller in case any covered system becomes defective *during the listing period*. These relatively inexpensive protection plans cost approximately $250 to $350 and are highly encouraged by real estate professionals who receive no compensation for recommending them to their clients.

Home warranty insurance plans normally cover such items as electrical wiring, heating, plumbing (portions of), the furnace, water heater, dishwasher, garbage disposal, toilet, central vacuum, and garage door opener units. Additional coverage may be purchased, at an added cost, for a swimming pool, spa, air conditioner, refrigerator, washer, dryer, and certain roof repairs.

Some sellers figure, especially in a hot real estate market, that they are better off to save the money and simply not bother providing a home warranty policy for a buyer. This logic is penny wise, and pound foolish, and sellers who persist with this thinking are not doing themselves a favor. ***One-year home warranties benefit both sellers and buyers.*** They can help prevent disputes, especially when the water heater breaks down or the dishwasher quits only days or weeks after the sale and the buyer blames the previous owner for concealing a problem.

If a system breaks after close of escrow, the buyer telephones a direct 1-800 line to the home warranty company, who then contacts a local repairperson with whom they have a repair contract. The repairperson then contacts the new homeowner to set up an appointment. The new owner pays a service fee of $35 or $50, depending on which plan was purchased. The home warranty company picks up the rest of the bill.

Having a warranty plan gives the buyer further assurance and additional confidence in the property he or she is purchasing. Sellers who provide home warranty protection plans let buyers know they have done their share to insure a happy and smooth transition regarding the mechanical aspects of homes — excellent benefits for a small price.

Use Home Inspections to Your Advantage

"We live among magnificent opportunities cleverly disguised as hopeless situations."

— Will Madden

Fred and Ethyl are proud of their home where they have lived for 15 years. Fred is the handy type and enjoys taking care of things around the house; he has always tried to make sure everything is in perfect working order. Over the years he's fixed everything and now he and Ethyl are moving to a retirement home. They like Henry, their real estate agent, and feel he has done a good job. Their home was listed for just 10 days when they received an excellent offer.

Henry had told them there would be a home inspection and this is standard procedure for buyers purchasing a home; but Fred is nervous about having an inspector come and poke around their house. He knows that despite its age, their place is in great shape. Henry has re-assured Fred the inspection will go well and suggested that Fred and Ethyl go out and have a nice lunch or see a movie while the inspector and the buyer are at the house.

Although Ethyl didn't think it was a good idea, Fred decided to stay through the entire inspection. The home inspector was a nice fellow, but Fred thought he was entirely too nosey. He

171

pointed out there were no GFI switches for safety near the sinks in the kitchen, bath, and laundry. He also noted an electric cord to the workbench in the garage was not properly wired, and several electric outlets had reverse polarity. By this time, Fred could feel his blood pressure rising.

The buyer was nice enough and stayed pretty quiet while the inspector went through the house. They all tried to make small talk to lighten the situation, but Fred felt awkward, embarrassed about some things that were said, and wished he had listened to his agent. Even though the great overall condition of their home was mentioned, he felt they didn't really appreciate all the work he had done. Fred was getting upset, and knew if he said what was really on his mind, he would probably anger both the inspector and the buyer. Henry was right… Fred and Ethyl should have gone to a movie.

The Home Inspection — You Won't Leave Home Without One

These days sellers need to be aware that almost every offer, one way or another will involve a home inspection on behalf of the buyers. Thankfully, this is the age of real estate disclosure, and buyers are strongly encouraged to have professional inspections of any property they intend to purchase. A home inspection can make the seller nervous, but for the buyer who is placing hundreds of thousands of dollars towards a home purchase, an inspection can save money on repairs and future litigation. Once the inspection is complete, the seller can contact the buyer's home inspector to explain any questionable findings or get clarification.

The American Society of Home Inspectors (ASHI) is the professional association representing the home inspection industry. ASHI has a code of ethics and enforces strict guidelines for its members. At the state level, the California Real Estate Inspection Association (CREIA) has existed since 1976. Many states are trying to raise the level of knowledge required of home inspectors and to maintain high standards of experience and integrity in this growing field.

These professional organizations test their members for minimum levels of construction knowledge and experience, and they require continuing education courses. Potential buyers are encouraged to contact their local contractor's licensing board for home inspector recommendations. At this time, CREIA (and most other state home inspection associations) are not regulated on either a national or a state level, meaning that *there is no licensing requirement for members*. Therefore, a home inspector's professional level of personal responsibility is not verifiable and the inspector is not legally accountable. ***It is important to understand that home inspectors are NOT necessarily licensed contractors.***

It is to the distinct advantage of both the wise buyer and smart seller to make sure the home inspector selected is a highly qualified professional; this means they have years of experience in the field of home building. The inspector's opinion (based on experience) should more than likely, be upheld in a court of law. *If an inspector is not qualified according to the following guidelines, find one who is.*

Verify that the home inspector:

☐ Belongs to either ASHI, or the state professional organization, or both.

☐ Has adequate liability insurance in case of on the job injury.

☐ Carries errors and omissions coverage in case they overlook something serious.

☐ Has many years of experience — the more the better.

☐ Is (preferably) a *licensed* contractor. Be sure the number of his license is on his business card and report forms.

During the professional home inspection, the seller may choose to stay on the premises and participate in the structural investigation. If you decide to stay, do not aggravate the inspector by hovering nearby or protesting the findings. You will only undermine your position and make the buyer's inspection process more difficult. If you want to have someone represent your interests, you may have your listing agent present for the home inspection. Your agent can relate a thorough account of the inspection and will provide you with a copy of the final report to review.

As mentioned earlier in Chapter 10 regarding Disclosure, you as a seller can hire your own home inspector. By taking the initiative on professional inspections, sellers can start building a foundation of honesty and trust with a potential buyer. Have a copy of the report available on the coffee table for potential buyers to study, and be prepared for your agent to discuss items listed in the report.

You can also contact your local utility company and request a *safety check* for any potential problems with gas and electrical connections. Utility personnel will gladly perform such an inspection and it is usually a free service that can provide you with a heads up regarding any heating, electrical, or appliance problem. It helps you to be more knowledgeable about the physical aspects of your property, and it will give you a chance to correct any health and safety issues before the inspector (or a potential buyer) knocks on your door.

Call in the Pros

From a practical standpoint for both seller and buyer, it is far better to have a professional home inspector than to hire a novice hoping to save money. Non-professionals are not legally accountable for their opinions, and if a question or dispute arises, the word of a professional is much more likely to be taken seriously by all concerned. Professional home inspectors have a standardized, printed format that takes them step-by-step through the various areas of the property. The time for an average inspection for an 1,800 square foot house might take three hours or more.

At this writing the cost of a typical home inspection, ranges between $250 and $300 and is usually paid for by the buyer, either directly to the home inspection company or through escrow. Larger and more complicated properties will have a higher inspection fee. Condominiums or residential units such as twin-homes will have prices that vary according to the square footage and complexity of the structure involved. When calling for a home inspection appointment, be ready to answer basic structural and square footage questions about your property in order to establish a quote for the final cost of your inspection.

The professional inspection report usually is comprised of at least a dozen pages and is broken down into the various structural areas of the property, including the home's exterior, garage, sunrooms, or attached conservatories. Usually a licensed roofing contractor examines roofs but not as part of a general home inspection. However, if the home inspector observes stains in the attic or ceiling areas, he may recommend further inspection by a roofing contractor. It is also very helpful and highly advisable to have the Pest Control Report on hand for the home inspector.

Professional home inspectors are part of most residential sales.

Of course, inspectors are not able to check inside walls and behind large pieces of furniture, but you can expect them to be very thorough. Electrical, plumbing, heating, and cooling systems are examined and major appliances are tested. If there is a fireplace, it will also be checked, and if anything unusual is noted, a fireplace or masonry contractor will be recommended to give a separate opinion. In the case of a home with a spa or swimming pool, a *licensed* pool technician should determine the condition of these systems and prepare a professional opinion of the equipment.

Dealing with the Home Inspection Report

After the home inspection has been completed, your listing agent will receive a copy of the report within several days. This may be accompanied by a written list of repairs the buyer is requesting. Depending on the contract negotiations, it helps a seller to bear in mind that these are only requests. *If a home inspection discovers any safety or health issues, usually the seller takes care of them.* Other requests, however, can be prioritized in order of importance, and, hopefully, will not become deal breakers. This is where real estate professionals shine and are usually able to negotiate an agreement that everyone can accept.

During these negotiating times, it is of the utmost importance to keep the bigger picture in mind and not lose sight of your overall goal: *to close escrow.* Try not to let egos or conflicting personalities get in the way of sound and logical business decisions. If the buyer's requests are reasonable, it is a good idea for you, the seller, to also be reasonable in negotiating any additional terms. Your agent will guide you in the areas you, as a seller, should stand firm and what areas are open to negotiation.

The Termite Report — Don't Bug Me!

The other major inspection (that can make or break a sale) concerns those annoying termites. Depending on where you live, damages resulting from termite infestation can be financially significant and more structurally invasive than most people realize. This is another part of the transaction that needs the focus and careful attention of the seller. In most states, nearly every residential real estate transaction will involve a Structural Pest Control Report, otherwise known as the termite report. The findings and any subsequent corrective repair work might involve hundreds if not thousands of dollars.

A termite report, in addition to assessing damages from these annoying critters, also identifies any *excessive moisture conditions* in and around the structure, such as dry rot, fungus damage, or mildew that can compromise the building's structural integrity. Inspectors look for signs of all these conditions and tag any suspicious areas they find needing corrective repair work.

Before putting a house on the market, smart sellers will order a termite inspection as early as possible so they know up front the estimated costs of any termite or moisture repairs. A report that confirms the presence of these conditions does not mean your home is less marketable, only that certain repairs are necessary in order to make it structurally sound before passing it on to a new buyer.

The costs involved with a termite report can be a negotiable item, but the seller usually takes responsibility for both the inspection itself and any subsequent repairs that result. Once any repairs are complete, the pest control operator certifies that the property is both free of termites and any adverse moisture conditions. This Certification of Completion is then filed with the Structural Pest Control Board in your state, sent to your escrow, then given to the buyer, and is available to the buyer's lender.

Judy and Bill were ready to put their home on the market, and Darlene, their listing agent, had suggested ways to make the house more appealing so it would sell quickly. During a preliminary meeting, Darlene told Judy and Bill they could count on a request from the buyer for a termite clearance. She wanted them to get a termite inspection done as soon as possible — preferably before the For Sale sign went up. She knew that having the termite report, showing what corrective work was needed and how much it would cost, could be a negotiating advantage if an offer came in early.

Since it often takes a while to schedule a termite inspection, Darlene advised Judy and Bill to make the appointment right away. Judy called three exterminator companies, but they were all so busy that an inspector would not be available for at least two weeks. The For Sale sign was set to go up on Monday morning, but all Judy and Bill could do was hope an offer requesting a termite clearance would not come in right away.

Because Judy and Bill needed a quick sale, they priced their home to move fast and did not add on a big percentage of profit. Bill felt nervous about both the home inspection and the termite report. The house was older, has had plumbing problems, and he thought there was probably some dry rot under the kitchen sink.

During her walk-through, Darlene recommended mostly minor fix-it tasks, such as repainting the front door, fixing a leaky faucet in the bathroom, and replacing a cracked bedroom window. Bill wanted to finish these small repair items before the termite and home inspectors arrived and was glad that Darlene had pointed them out.

On Monday morning, Darlene had arranged for the For Sale sign to be placed in the front yard, and by mid-afternoon several neighbors called wondering why Judy and Bill were moving and inquired about their price. Several days later they received an offer from a buyer who came fairly close to their asking price. The buyer wanted Judy and Bill to provide a pest control clearance; the offer also stated the buyers would have a home inspection at the buyer's expense. The buyer could close escrow in 45 days and was well qualified for a new loan. With the exception of being a little short on price, Darlene said she felt it was a good offer.

Judy and Bill were pleased with the potential contract, but the buyer's agent had indicated his clients had come in with their best offer and would not be able to go any higher. The pest control company was not coming for another week, and Judy and Bill did not know what the final termite repair costs would be. Their home was over thirty years old and would probably need a total fumigation, which meant tenting the structure in order to obtain a pest control clearance. They realized various other repairs could be even more costly.

As Judy and Bill sat with Darlene to respond to the offer, they felt the $3,000 potential termite repair bill would cut their proceeds too low, especially since these clients could not come up any higher in price to offset Judy and Bill's termite expense. Not wanting to take a chance on excessive corrective work and coming up financially short, they decided to wait for another offer. Disappointed, they felt they had no choice but to let this buyer go and wait to see what turned up in the termite inspection.

Schedule Early for Smart Negotiating

Judy and Bill experienced what happens when a seller does not have a termite report in their hands when an offer comes in: they found themselves in a poor bargaining position. ***Sellers need to schedule a report early so they can figure that cost into their bottom-line proceeds.*** Without knowing that net amount, an owner is counter-offering blind and must simply hope for the best when the termite report finally does come in.

A seller will eventually need to have a pest control report made anyway, and waiting until an offer is on the table is too late to help in negotiations. As of this writing, the cost for a residential termite inspection for an 1,800 sq. ft. home is approximately $100. If your funds are limited, this bill can be deducted from your escrow proceeds when the house sells. This should make it easier to get your inspection done as soon as the decision to sell is definite.

A Pest Control Report is usually valid for six months and becomes part of the disclosure items for the property (refer to Chapter 10). Having a recent termite report is like having an extra ace in the seller's hand. Especially in a quick escrow, it can save precious days, and many headaches by paving the way for a smoother sale. To schedule an inspection, the owner or the owner's listing agent (at their request) will call a reputable, licensed pest control company and schedule an appointment to make a thorough inspection of the house, both inside and out. The pest control operator will go through the home and garage, up into the attic, and into the basement or crawl space, if there is one.

I strongly encourage the seller to be present during this termite inspection because you can ask questions and get a first-hand idea of the condition of your property. After the inspection, a written report is prepared and mailed to the property owner and the listing agent within about a week.

Because the termite report may seem technical, the listing agent and the seller can review the report together. It is important to understand what is required, especially if the repair work is sizeable. Be sure to read the fine print of your report carefully. Do not hesitate to ask questions and get satisfactory answers from the company that made the report. A reputable pest control operator will help clarify the technical jargon.

Another reason to get an early report is that home inspectors often want the termite report in their hands when inspecting the property — this helps them not overlook anything and to do a more thorough job. If the home inspector finds additional problems that were not discovered in the termite inspection, a termite company with a good reputation will return and do further investigation. Since you have everything to gain, be diligent and follow up.

What *They* See Is What *You* Get

Be aware that home inspections and termite reports will be based only on what areas are *visible* and available for inspection. *Inaccessible areas, such as garages full of boxes or the insides of walls, are not covered,* and the fine print of the report makes this clear. This is an important distinction since termites, moisture, or other structural problems are often found *inside* walls and in places that are hard to see.

Inspectors look for tell-tale signs of structural problems and termites, such as droppings or termite wings, but stop short at tearing up floors and carpeting and moving heavy furniture and appliances. Since most inspections are made while the house is occupied and filled with the owner's belongings, it is often physically impossible to see everything that might be a problem.

Knowledgeable real estate agents in states where termites are especially prevalent, such as California, Hawaii, and Florida, know that getting a pest control clearance may make the difference between selling a listing and having an escrow cancel. An experienced professional will guide a seller through the maze of finding a reputable termite company, understanding the report terminology, and determining what corrective work is necessary.

Distinguishing Section I and Section II Items on a Report

The findings and recommendations outlined in a pest control report are classified under the headings of Section I and Section II. ***Any corrective work classified as Section I refers to an active, ongoing insect infestation or moisture condition.*** In order to obtain a *clearance*, these areas will be treated with pesticides or corrected by whatever means are called for in the report recommendations. Examples of persistent insects would include drywood swarmers (of the order *Isoptera* that feeds on wood), dampwood termites, subterranean termites (a different type of termite that goes underground and is especially damaging to a substructure), and wood-boring beetles.

Moisture conditions classified as Section I items might be areas where dry rot, fungus, active mold, or mildew are present. Often found in the attic, roof sheathing, attached decking, or handrails, dry rot can also lurk under sinks and sub-floors around toilets, showers, and bathtubs. These repairs must also be corrected before a certification of clearance is issued.

Section II items are conditions that are not of a serious nature at present, but could lead to a potential Section I condition if left untreated. Examples of these might be cellulose debris under the house (wood scraps left under the raised foundation when the house was built) and areas near shower or tub enclosures where water drips, leading to eventual dry rot or damaged wallboard.

Often a buyer will not require the clearance of the relatively minor Section II items, understanding that the real task is to clear

Section I recommendations. However, it is important to know that government-approved loans, such as FHA and VA, will require a complete clearance of both Sections I and II. In many years of selling property, I have seen numerous transactions come perilously close to falling apart due to the high cost of clearing a termite report. As a seller, you'll be far better off getting your report as early as possible; then you'll know what your cost will be to obtain that clear certification.

Don't Hesitate to Renegotiate

Sometimes a seller will insist on delaying a termite report until after they receive an offer, perhaps because they do not want it to be part of early disclosure items, thereby discouraging a buyer with difficult information. However, if an escrow is going to be cancelled over something in the termite report, why wait until the last minute to get the bad news? Better to bite the bullet, negotiate if possible, and not waste precious weeks hoping the worst will not happen.

You can do some of the corrective work early in the listing period to mitigate what you know will be required work later. Another option on a large termite repair bill is to re-negotiate and lower the price so the buyer can make his own choices about what termite work is important to him, what is absolutely required, and what is optional. If the lender's appraisal calls for a clear pest control report as a condition of the new loan, *neither you nor the buyer will have any say in the matter.* However, if the appraisal did not stipulate a termite clearance, you have options. Here again, your agent will guide you.

If the buyer really wants your home, the presence of termites will probably not prevent a sale. Major problems would probably have shown up somewhere else (for example, on a home inspection report or the listing agent's disclosure walk-through). Remember, as with the price of the initial report, the cost of pest control repairs can be paid for out of the escrow proceeds and does not need to come out of a seller's pocket immediately.

A Pest Maintenance Program Does Not Ensure a Clear Report

Often a property owner has contracted for an on-going, periodic pest control service performed monthly or quarterly in and around the house to keep spiders, sowbugs, earwigs, and other bugs in check. *Think of this as a bug maintenance program only.* It is not necessarily controlling termite damage or hidden dry-rot problems. A pest control clearance for a sale or loan refinance is *much more thorough*. Do not confuse the two.

Members of the termite family are elusive, powerful for their size, and hungry. Over time, termites can cause tremendous structural damage to a house. Real estate agents sometimes joke about older homes in California being kept together solely by the termites holding hands! Where these pests are prevalent, we deal with their consequences almost daily. A very experienced pest control operator once told me, "I can fumigate a house on Monday, and on Thursday a cloud of dry-wood swarmers can come and settle in. Tenting only takes care of what is present when the tarp goes over the house."

186

*Termite inspectors report visible infestations
and moisture conditions.*

The Wet Ones: Mold, Mildew, and Dry Rot

As mentioned earlier, the termite report deals with more than just bugs. As a seller, it helps to know that this inspection will also locate and identify any existing, or potential, moisture condition (fungus, mold, mildew, and dry rot) present in the structure. Typical locations for moisture problems are under sinks and around shower and bathtub enclosures where a shower door or curtain does not fit snugly so water splashes onto the nearby wall and the floor. If this condition is not corrected, the moisture can seep through old grout and get behind walls or erode the wood sub-floor. This process takes years and happens so slowly the occupants of the home may not notice it.

Any discoloration, change in texture, or bubbling of the wallboard can be evidence of adverse moisture conditions. Darkening linoleum may indicate wetness and dry rot in the sub-floor. A soft or spongy feeling, especially around the base of toilets, is another indicator. The only solution, when dry rot has gone this far, is to replace the rotted wood and/or wallboard. An ounce of prevention in cases like these is worth a pound of cure. However, once the damage is done, it needs to be fixed.

To Tent or Not to Tent —
That is the Question

Unfortunately, termite infestation and damage will often reach into inaccessible locations of a home, such as roof sheathing, eaves, and attic areas that cannot be corrected by localized or spot pesticide treatment. To comply with the purchase contract or the lender's demands, the building may have to be tented and fumigated with a powerful pesticide, usually "Vikane™" (a trade name for sulfuryl fluoride).

The long-term effects of fumigation on people and pets are still being studied. However, young children, the elderly, or anyone with asthma, respiratory ailments, or chemical sensitivities may find the fumigation process particularly noxious, and have adverse health reactions if they move back into a fumigated structure too soon. Usually, several days of airing out after the tent comes off is sufficient for these chemicals to dissipate. However, I strongly encourage fumigation to be scheduled for the last few days of escrow, even if the owners need to stay in a motel for a short time. Try not to return to a fumigated structure, and if possible, arrange for this procedure to be done after you have moved out completely.

Be sure to read the disclaimers on the pest control report that pertain to the use of these powerful chemicals. Heed their warnings and take the necessary precautions. If food is present in the house during tenting, special plastic covering and sealing is absolutely necessary and is usually provided by the fumigation company. The refrigerator's contents must be tightly sealed with strong tape and all boxes of cereals and grains in pantry areas need to be protected.

When any pesticide is applied for the treatment of termites or other wood-boring insects, the occupants and owner are required to sign a statement that they are aware of the chemicals being used and the risks involved. In California, pesticide disclosure is required by law, and termite/fumigation companies must comply with strict regulations. You can see why it is far better to have an empty property fumigated after the occupants and their belongings are gone.

Unfortunately, some of the loveliest plants surrounding a home can be damaged or killed when the structure is tented. During this process it is very difficult to adequately protect the vegetation close to the structure from exposure to the lethal gas. Although workers try to be careful when securing the huge tent over the entire structure, it is unavoidable that they step on and often damage shrubs that grow right next to the house. However, buyers and sellers now have choices, and it is not absolutely necessary to tent and fumigate with powerful pesticides to obtain a pest control clearance and certification.

Alternatives to Fumigation:
Br-r-r-r, Ouch, and Zap!

In recent years, other alternatives to fumigation have become available for termite-infested buildings. These techniques involve freezing, very high temperatures, and/or electrocution. The termites may not agree, but below-zero temperatures, extreme heat, or high voltage electricity is gentler to the house and surrounding foliage than the use of strong pesticides. To find out more about these environmentally friendly possibilities, check your local phone book or ask your real estate agent for names of companies using these methods. These kinder alternatives to rid your home of termites are financially competitive with the pesticide method. Both alternatives provide similar guarantees and time frames for keeping the pests at bay.

Eliminating termites by freezing, heat treatment, or electrocution works in a more specific, localized way and will not kill plants or leave pesticide residues. Companies that offer this alternative service are also regulated by the state and must comply with the same standards that apply to traditional pesticide-using termite companies. Banks and lenders will also honor a clearance from them. In fact, a buyer who realizes that these alternatives exist may well find these newer choices the best solution for health and environmental reasons. Knowing that you have options will provide greater flexibility when it comes to making decisions about eliminating termites that will satisfy both your buyer and the purchase contract.

SOLD! Closing the Escrow and Moving On

"To sell a house is to walk away from a cluster of memories; to buy it is to choose where the future will take place."

— *"Under the Tuscan Sun,"* Frances Mayes

Jeane and Bob are in the last stages of selling their home. Escrow closes in a week and they are anxiously finishing up the last details for their move. Although Carol Anne, their listing agent, told them, "It's not sold until the deed is recorded in the new buyer's name," the reality of the physical move started to sink in. Bob, being a very thorough seller, has verified with the escrow officer that the buyer's funds are ready, and that their loan is set to fund. The pest control company has sent the certificate of completion to the escrow office, and Bob finished the last few repairs he needed to make around the house.

Jeane and Bob know they have been very fortunate. The buyers, a delightful young family, love their home and will take good care of the property. All those years of tending the rose garden, fruit trees, and herbs were worth the effort; the new owners will thoroughly enjoy them.

Jeane is having mixed emotions. Although she is happy at the thought of moving closer to her mother and being in a lovely new house, she realizes more each day that she is very sad to leave this place where she has good friends and wonderful memories. This is where they brought their children home from the hospital, held all the birthday parties, hunted for Easter eggs in the yard, hosted their daughter's engagement party, and enjoyed all the Christmas seasons with the tree in the front bay window.

Although Jeane's friends have assured her they will stay in touch, she knows that many of her dearest associations will fade away. Still, she and Bob have agreed that this move is necessary for his work and that it will bring Jeane much closer to her aging mother. Bob says that he will miss this place, but he is ready to move on. He looks forward to the large garage and work area in their new house, yet Jeane knows she will miss this home a lot. They are especially grateful for Carol Anne's suggestion during the negotiations that they add another week to the escrow period since all the last minute details have become so time consuming.

Joyce, a dear old friend, is coming over today to help Jeane wrap the dishes and glassware. Joyce is the perfect one to help carefully box up all the kitchen perishables, and Jeane will be grateful for the company. On the day escrow closes, Bob intends to mow the lawn for the last time. Jeane knows that she will somehow be ready to go when moving day arrives.

Why Escrow?

Escrow adds a neutral third party to real estate transactions. Escrow officers act upon previously agreed instructions from both buyer and seller. During escrow, the seller and buyer formalize their agreement to mutually sell and purchase a piece of real property. The escrow officer is the person in charge of a particular real estate transaction and the corresponding escrow file. He or she is responsible for preparing, handling, and recording all the documents, including the grant deed that formalizes the transfer of ownership.

Many areas throughout the country use attorneys rather than escrow officers to handle the transfer of real estate from a seller to a buyer. However, using escrow services seems to be growing in popularity nationwide. Escrow can be as simple as transferring a title or as complex as coordinating all the paperwork involved in the sale of a home, a parcel of land, a business, or a shopping center.

Escrow, especially useful because of its *neutrality*, only acts upon directions from both buyer and seller. In states where escrow is used, this process handles and organizes all the details of a multi-page purchase contract, the paperwork dealing with transfer of title, the funding of the new loan, and the paying off of the old one. Escrow officers process disclosure forms, termite reports, home inspections, rental agreements, former deeds of all kinds, and a host of other complicated documents necessary to pass ownership from a seller to a buyer.

Most large cities will have many excellent independent escrow companies, but the escrow office and the title company may often be one and the same. Sellers and buyers want to choose an established escrow company that has been in business for many years and has a solid reputation. Here again, your agent will guide you. Because it is so helpful to understand the escrow process, please refer to *The Life of an Escrow* in Appendix F for a flowchart of how an escrow proceeds.

The escrow officer keeps your file organized, making sure everybody gets what they need when they need it.

Professional real estate brokers and agents know the value of a good escrow officer, and most would agree that experienced ones are invaluable. Their responsibilities and duties are intense. They must be capable of handling countless legal details regarding many transactions simultaneously and be alert to a potential problem in a loan or a title issue. They will then notify the agents who can often resolve these issues without the buyer and seller becoming involved. When working with customers in sometimes stress-filled circumstances, escrow officers need patience, tolerance, and a sense of humor. Try to remember that the escrow staff is on your side and deserves to be treated with respect and courtesy even if something goes wrong or if paperwork is a bit late.

Achieving a Seamless Move

The death of a loved one, divorce, and moving, in that order, are said to be the three greatest stresses we will experience in life Whether you are moving across the street or across the country, relocating yourself and your family can be very hard work — physically and emotionally. Because of all the potential breakage and damage involved in a move, the jokes abound: "Three big moves are comparable to having a good fire."

Years ago families lived in the same house for generations; the home was the family seat. Babies were born under its roof, grandparents would die there, and most of life's important events took place within those special walls. The family home served as a refuge from all the ups and downs that life might bring.

Over the last seventy-five years, and especially after World War II, the permanence of home and family has changed dramatically. In our highly mobile society, not only are people leaving rural areas to seek work in the cities, but job changes and divorces occur much more frequently. Moving our physical location has become a continuous fact of life. Eventually, most of us can expect to relocate our possessions to a new place *at least* half a dozen times during our lifetime.

People in the military, or anyone in a highly transitional job, may move six or more times within a decade! This, added to the faster daily pace of life, increases our already high stress levels and challenges even the most tranquil of spirits. More than ever, we need the balance, harmony, and serenity that feng shui principles can provide as we move from place to place.

Be Smart and Move Slowly

After you prepare your home, using all the feng shui and real estate suggestions to help you sell quickly that are discussed in Chapters 4 through 11, your listing agent will shortly be bringing you a purchase offer. In your real estate negotiations, know that settling on the length of escrow (how long the process will take to transfer title to the new owner) is not always a simple decision. Be sure to consider carefully the length of escrow before signing.

Since this book is designed to be helpful for sellers, you should know that trying to speed up the closure can be a stressful mistake. Often, owners do not realistically assess all the physical work and details that lay ahead in the transition. If you want your move to be smooth, you need to give yourself adequate time to prepare. If you shortchange your move-out period, you will pay the price in headaches and wish you had given yourself more time. If at all possible in your negotiations, ask for at least one additional week of escrow time.

Usually, the last week before close of escrow is filled with the hectic final details including packing, endlessly labeling boxes, and discarding what you aren't taking with you. You also must notify the post office of your new address, shut down utility services at your current residence, establish new services at your next house, make countless phone calls, care for traumatized pets, and have school files transferred. People do not go through this challenging process for fun. Moving is expensive and the cost of packing, transporting, and possibly storing furniture, household goods, clothing, tools, and appliances can cost thousands of dollars.

Moving out of a house can be frantic or very manageable, depending on how you go about it. The variable factor here is having sufficient time, as well as *using time wisely.* Moving can also be productive in that it provides the opportunity to get rid of things you find unnecessary to take with you to your new home. Feng shui teaches us to make conscious choices, to be clear in our intentions, to proceed with care, and try to keep everything in balance in the process.

Involve the Children — They Can Help

Most children over the age of seven or eight can be given a fair share of responsibilities with the family move, especially if they understand that their carefully packed belongings will reappear unbroken in their new home. Provide them with enough boxes, wrapping paper, and marking pens or crayons. If given careful directions, they should be quite capable of boxing up their own toys, books, and clothing. They can even label each container correctly with pictures, if not words.

This is a great chance to *get youngsters in the habit of paring down.* Help them understand that they do not have to take it all with them to their next home. Garage sales are for children, too. They can sell old toys and clothes that no longer fit. Use this opportunity to teach your children the feng shui principle of taking to their new bedroom only what brings them joy and makes their heart smile. The rest can be passed on to other young folks who will benefit and receive delight from the items that your children no longer need.

Saying "Goodbye" and "Thank You"

Sometimes a seller will have only lived in a property for a short time and may not feel any sadness when leaving. However, when a family has lived in a home for many years and has emotionally bonded with it, as Bob and Jeane have, they can experience feelings of grief and separation when the time comes to leave. This is not unusual. It is something like saying farewell to an old friend you know you may not see again.

Although it might be easier to ignore these feelings, feng shui shows us it is much healthier to admit that our feelings are real and deal with them in productive and healing ways. Acknowledging the existence of our emotions is the first step. Omitting this phase of the moving process is like painting a picture without first outlining the subject: there is no focus, the work is haphazard, and the results may be disappointing or shallow. Our goal is balance as we go through the re-location process. We appreciate and acknowledge the old as we move on and prepare for the new.

Just as a mature plant will undergo some transplant shock when dug up and moved to a new location in the garden, most of us have difficulty leaving an environment where we have put down our own roots. The deeper these roots, the greater our feelings of separation when leaving a beloved space. During a move, children (especially teenagers whose peer group is their support) may feel sad, moody, angry, or withdrawn. This is a very natural reaction, and handling these feelings properly can make all the difference for them and for the entire family.

At this time it can be of great help to talk openly about what each family member is feeling and whatever misgivings, if any, they are experiencing. Everyone can benefit from discussing the thoughts and emotions they have during the packing and moving preparations, especially younger children who may not completely understand all that is going on.

Children simply know they are abandoning their bedroom and cannot remember ever being anywhere else. They may have to say goodbye to that special hiding place in the yard, and more importantly, to their favorite friend down the street. Feelings might be uncovered such as, "I'm really going to miss this neighborhood. It will be sad not to be with all our friends," and "Moving so far away will feel so different. I wonder if the people in our new place will be as wonderful as our friends here?" and even, "I hope our garden, where we've spent so much time, will be taken care of." All these thoughts are very real, and it will help if they are expressed and acknowledged by the family. If it is hard to say these words, at least *write* them down. The main idea is to be in touch with these feelings and then be able to move on in a more spiritually graceful and balanced way.

Moving Along With the Highest Intentions

If you and your family have lived in a particular home for a long time and feel bonded with the house, there is nothing wrong with having a little farewell party for yourselves. Also, celebrate the home you are leaving and the friends who have shared that special space with each of you. If you feel a bit shy about this, you can accomplish it in a very private way.

An example of this might be to arrange a simple gathering. Turn the telephone off, then stand together in the living room while you light a candle. With each person recalling a special memory of the house, essentially thank the home for all the joy and delight you have experienced. This small ritual step will help bring closure to the physical act of uprooting and moving on. It does not need to be a time of maudlin or sad feelings; make it a gesture of gratitude to the space that has given you so much.

Native Americans will smudge a home or teepee with special cleansing herbs such as white sage or sweetgrass before passing it along to a new family. Most owners today will clean the cupboards and sweep the floors before leaving a house. Remember Golda in *Fiddler on the Roof* who felt she needed to sweep the floors even as the family was being driven out of their village of Anatevka? What Tevia didn't seem to understand as he watched his wife using the broom, was that she knew that this important act reflected on her and made her feel better as the family left their home of so many years.

The act of energetically cleansing the space and sweeping it clean, prepares it in an *honorable way* for the new occupant. This parting gesture seems to reflect on us and how we pay attention to final details involving the home we are passing on to another. It is not a trivial exercise, and it deserves our time and respect.

Another example that will give a sense of closure to a particular space is to take a few minutes to quietly stand in each room, savoring it in a special way for the last time. Let the essence of each room surround you and seep into your spirit as you recall the memories that the space holds. *Try to dwell only on the good thoughts and let the difficult ones go.* This exercise may take only fifteen or twenty minutes as you walk through the entire house, but the short time spent will go a long way toward helping you to fully move out. You can let go of a beloved home in a way that will serve you well, and that should help prepare you for what lies ahead in the dwelling that is to be your new sacred space.

Final thoughts...

"Serenely we must pass through every mansion, clinging to some as to a beloved native land; the living spirit is no fettering hand, from step to step it leads us toward expansion."

— Herman Hesse

So often as I help clients sell their homes and offer feng shui suggestions, they will say to me, "Why haven't I thought of doing this long ago... it's all so simple? Why now, when I am selling my home, am I preparing it for someone else to live in happily? I could have been enjoying it this way all along."

Why should we only use these feng shui ideas of balance and harmony for our environment when getting ready to leave our home? It is my hope you will use at least some of the suggestions in this book to help get your home sold more quickly, if that is your decision. *I would also invite you to consider using this philosophy to prepare your home for delightful living now.* Remember that this is your life and not merely a rehearsal. Why not experience it to the fullest and highest potential?

Feng shui teaches us how to savor our home on a higher level, and to live intentionally surrounded only by what brings us joy and makes our hearts smile. I hope each of you will consider the enormous potential of this information and use it — to fully savor your sacred space.

May the power of feng shui enrich you and your family each day, in every possible way.

Namaste, Holly Ziegler

Appendices

Appendix A:
Compass School *Pa kua*

Fame
South
Middle Daughter
Red
Fire

Wealth
Southeast
Eldest Daughter
Purple
Wood

Relationships
Southwest
Mother
Pink
Earth

HEALTH &
WELL-BEING

Family
East
Eldest Son
Green
Wood

Children
West
Youngest Daughter
White
Metal

Yellow
EARTH

Knowledge
Northeast
Youngest Son
Turquoise
Earth

Career
North
Middle Son
Black
Water

Helpful People
Northwest
Father
Gray
Metal

Appendix B:
BTB School Bagua

BTB Bagua Over Simple Floor Plan

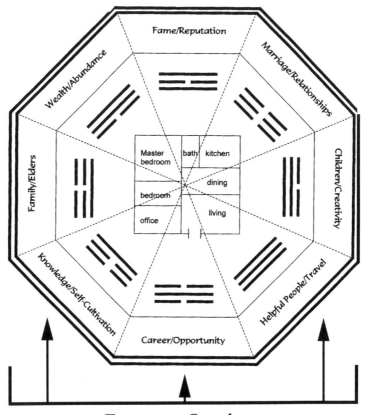

Fame/Reputation

Wealth/Abundance

Marriage/Relationships

Family/Elders

Children/Creativity

Knowledge/Self-Cultivation

Helpful People/Travel

Career/Opportunity

Master bedroom | bath | kitchen
dining
bedroom
living
office

Entrance Quadrant
(Front door is in one of these three positions)

Appendix C:
Feng Shui Remedies and
The Real Estate Cure

Feng shui remedies, or solutions, are put into place in order to affect the chi, or correct a negative condition within a space. Remedies are also called cures, and can be chi *activators, adjusters, enhancers, stimulators, lifters, stabilizers, or deflectors,* depending upon the correction needed. When placing feng shui remedies, it is especially important to remember that they are to be put in place with a sincere heart while setting a clear intention.

An example of setting an intention would be: "As I light this candle in my entryway, I want to welcome the new buyer into my home." Intentions are spoken aloud, using a prayer-like hand gesture, and focusing the mind clearly on the goal itself. For best results, setting the intention is then followed by a simple prayer of choice, such as the Lord's Prayer, O Man I Pad Me Hum mantra, or whatever feels appropriate for the person setting the cure in place.

Reflective or Refractive Objects

(deflect and send chi away)
mirrors
crystals
lights

Moving Objects

(disperse/raise chi)
windsocks
whirly-gigs
fountains
wind chimes

fans
flag mobiles

Moving Water

(attracts chi)
fountains
waterfalls
aquariums

Energy Producing Objects

(amplifies or stimulates chi)
appliances, fireplaces
computers
candles, incense

Sound Producing

(attract chi)
wind chimes
fountains
music

Weighty Objects

(solidify and stabilize chi)
statues
rocks, boulders
benches

Traditional Chinese Cures

bagua mirror	protection, deflect sha chi
bamboo flutes	protection, longevity
fu dogs	protection
gourds	fertility, abundance
talismans	protection, blessings
coins	abundance, wealth
fish	abundance

The Feng Shui Real Estate Cure

When first writing this book, I intended to stay with only the very practical side of feng shui that would help owners sell their houses faster. This basic knowledge, and the methods given, would provide more than sufficient means to get the job done. However, throughout the course of this project, I have come to the conclusion that many readers might want a higher level of feng shui knowledge, and omitting it, would be a true disservice to those who do.

This more transcendental, prayer-like method or cure takes feng shui to the next level. This higher, intentional, and more spiritual distinction of feng shui, like anything non-scientific, requires faith, firm purpose, and a willingness to be open-minded. Anyone not wanting this more advanced level cure, may consider it superstition and choose to ignore it. I will say, however, that its use has had an extremely high rate of success.

I invite those of you who would like to give it a try, to do so with complete confidence, deep respect, and most of all, a sincere heart. The Real Estate Cure can be used for selling a home or a business. ***Naturally, it is vital that the property be priced appropriately for current market conditions.*** (Pricing is a mundane, physical, or worldly step.) The cure outlined below is the transcendental method to move energy in the direction of a successful sale and is shared through the generosity of the benevolent H.H. Grand Master Lin Yun.

A. Remove something small from the house that had to do with the construction or is structural in nature, such as a small piece of tile, a switch plate screw, or a nail. It should be something that can easily be replaced and will not be noticeable afterwards.

B. Place this small item in a red envelope. Take this item to a river or stream, preferably between the hours of 11 am and 1 pm (which is the most yang and powerful time of day). The faster the current the better.

C. Throw the item into the water and visualize letting go of the house. This active visualization aspect is most important and is the main focus of this exercise. With your hands in a prayer-like attitude, speak aloud your intention that you are ready to leave your home and want the right buyer to come as soon as possible. Give this your fullest attention of mind and sincerity of heart.

D. Your home will make someone very happy. Visualize the right buyer *catching up* with your house. This mental imaging should visualize a win-win situation for both parties. Everyone gets what they want, the transaction goes smoothly and the outcome is positive for all involved.

E. Just after escrow closes and you are ready to vacate, replace the piece that was removed with a new one.

In ancient Chinese feng shui, within the Black Tantric Buddhist Sect, there is a solemn practice of honoring the *tradition of the red envelope.* Whenever a transcendental feng shui cure is passed from teacher to student, in keeping with this tradition, the student gives to the instructor a token of appreciation placed inside a red envelope. Red is the color of power and symbolizes the flame of knowledge and wisdom. The token of appreciation can be monetary or anything of appreciation which would fit the occasion.

This honoring of the red envelope is not about money, but rather of an *energetic* nature… it protects the lineage of the chi within the cure, and further protects the chi of the giver of the knowledge. Symbolically the envelope acts like a shield, and is considered not only proper, but also necessary to the process of sharing transcendental information.

This transcendental real estate cure for selling a house comes directly from H.H. Grand Master Professor Lin Yun, and is shared here for your benefit with his permission. ***My request is: If you use this transcendental method of getting your house sold, place a token of your appreciation inside a red envelope and send it to Professor Lin Yun.*** Proceeds will be used for educational and charitable purposes. Please accept my sincere gratitude in advance for honoring this tradition.

H.H. Grand Master Prof. Lin Yun
Yun Lin Temple
2959 Russell Street
Berkeley, CA 94705

Appendix D: Significance of Colors and Numbers

Colors

As professor Lin Yun has said, "...color defines for us what exists and what does not exist. (It) discloses the status of one's health... inspires emotion...and structures our behavior." [18] It affects our moods and alters our perception of space within an environment. In feng shui, color plays a significant role in implementation of solutions to challenges both in interior design and outside the home in landscaping. Color is tied to the cycles of the 5 Elements, and each element has its associated hue.

Red: *Fire Element*, happiness, power, luck, passion, fame, aggression, summer.

Yellow: *Earth Element*, stability, royalty, gaiety, patience, wisdom, autumn.

Orange: happiness, power, autumn.

Green: *Wood Element*, growth, inspiration, re-birth, eternity, harmony, spring

Blue: *Water Element*, heaven, clarity of communication, spirituality, winter

Purple: high office, wealth, power, richness, spirituality

---

[18] Grand Master Lin Yun & Sarah Rossbach, *Living Color*, p.11

Grey: *Metal Element*, ambivalence, frustration, ambiguity, hopelessness.

White: *Metal Element*, purity, precision, rigidity, (in China used for mourning).

Black: *Water Element*, spirituality, intellectual depth, continuity, wisdom, winter.

Brown: *Earth Element*, stability, depth, endurance, autumn

Gold: *Metal Element*, richness, power

Numbers

Numbers are highly significant in feng shui, and in China numbers play an important role in selection of addresses, choosing of license plates, and determining dates for significant events such as the opening of a business. Numbers are symbolic of lucky associations with words that have similar sounds.

Yin numbers are even, and yang numbers are odd. In general, yang numbers are considered more fortunate than those that are yin. In Chinese hotels, it is not uncommon to be missing the 4th floor, while in the West, often the 13th floor is omitted! When considering an address, numbers are added together until the final result is less than 10.

For example - 2874 Easy Street would be figured as follows:

$$2 + 8 = 10, +7 = 17 + 4 = 21. 2 + 1 = 3$$

Zero: represents perfection, completion, and harmony.

One: in Chinese the word for one sounds like the word for honor… considered lucky; represents the Water element and the direction of north.

Two: sounds similar to the word for sure. Two stands for *doubling up* as in *multiplying your happiness* and is considered a good number. It corresponds with Fire and south.

Three: sounds like the word for growth, or alive and is considered lucky; represents Wood and east.

Four: very similar to the word for death and felt to be very unlucky unless combined with a favorable number such as 45. Four represents the west direction and the Metal element.

Five: represents the central Bagua position (also on the lo-shu Magic Square) and signifies balance; when combined with 2, 4, 6, or 8, it becomes extremely auspicious, because each pair of numbers is balanced.

Six: sounds like the word for *wealth*, making it very popular. Represents the Water element and the direction of north.

Seven: also sounds like the word for *sure*, and is considered to be a very fortunate number; represents Fire and south.

Eight: similar to the word *multiply* and is extremely lucky; considered to be a fertile number, so if you desire many children, live in a house with this address; represents the Wood element and the east direction.

Nine: considered to be one of the luckiest numbers because it sounds like the word for longevity and long life; is the highest of the single digit, whole numbers; represents the Metal element and the west direction. [19]

---

[19] Angel Thompson, *Feng Shui – How to Achieve the Most Harmonious Arrangement of your Home & Office*. p. 71

Appendix E: Case Histories

From Ila Hamilton, Real Estate Broker, Century 21 Filer, Pismo Beach, California:

A woman came up to me after attending one of my feng shui seminars, and asked for a private consultation. Her home had been listed with a broker for over a year, and was getting no activity. She told me that the listing had expired, she was in poor health, and her husband was in a wheelchair. They desperately needed help getting their house sold.

When I arrived at their home, the entry was filled with large, overgrown plants, some of which were dead, and most only barely alive. Each room was filled with collections of all sorts, and every table was filled with "stuff." In order to watch television during the day, in a second bedroom, they had placed cardboard over the windows.

The family room was paneled with dark wood and had heavy dark ceiling beams. There were several large, overstuffed chairs that she told me were never used; one bedroom was filled with her sewing and craft items that she didn't work on anymore.

I told them that if they really wanted to get their house sold, some changes would need to be made, and with their permission, I would help them get the house in shape. I started with the plants in the entry, taking away all the dead and sick ones, replacing them with flowers in vibrant colors. My son came over to help them box up all the collections and put the boxes in the garage.

I had the beams painted off-white to match new light wallpaper, I removed the cardboard from the window, placed the television in the closet, and arranged the furniture so that they could both enjoy the room and watch TV.

All this took about two weeks to accomplish. Three weeks later the house was in escrow. I then sold them a great single-level condo, and when they moved, I helped them get rid of all their excess stuff. Since then this nice couple has since sent me numerous referral clients.

Ila Hamilton is a Broker-Associate with Century 21 Filer Realtors, Pismo Beach, California. She is a licensed building contractor (#412846), Professional member of ASID, a Certified Interior Designer in the state of California, and feng shui consultant.

From James Jay, BTB Feng Shui consultant and teacher, Nevada City, California:

It was a sweltering August night. The kind of night you remember from childhood when you couldn't sleep because your pillow was so hot that your head felt like it would explode if it got any hotter. The kind of night that makes you uncomfortable no matter what you do and no fan will take the edge off. The kind of night that has air so thick it feels like there's a brace constricting your chest every time you take a breath.

On such a night my wife Helen and I received a phone call. It was a client named Lila. Lila pleaded with us to come over the next day because she needed a feng shui adjustment as soon as humanly possible. It seems she had found herself suddenly in a new place and felt that the vibes weren't quite right. The problem was, only weeks before, Lila was in another home, a home that Helen and I had already worked on. Although the place felt great Lila still wasn't happy in that home. It was too much house for her and her young daughter. She wanted to downsize.

Lila had put her house on the market months before. It was a high rent house in a low rent town and she had few lookers. She called to ask us if there were any feng shui cures for selling real estate. Helen and I replied that there was indeed a powerful cure that we had learned from our teacher, Grandmaster Lin Yun. Most feng shui cures contain two elements, the mundane and the transcendental. On the mundane level, one must do everything logically possible to affect the desired result and when that didn't achieve results then the transcendental would be invoked.

In Lila's case, she had done the mundane work. She made sure the house was priced fairly for the market she was in. She did the advertising, listed the house, engaged a real estate sales agent and held open houses whenever possible. The people just weren't coming.

We offered Lila the Real Estate Cure which consisted of the ceremonial use of a red envelope in a simple ritual along with her sincere intention. Lila performed the ceremony and was astonished that, no more than a week after performing it, a buyer came along who absolutely loved the house. He even offered her the asking price! Suddenly, Lila needed to find a residence and rented her current abode.

During these dog days of summer, Lila found that her current house was lacking in balance and harmony and hence the need call to us that hot night. We made arrangements to see her the next day at which time we walked through her place offering feng shui suggestions. She kept shaking her head every time she thought about how fast the sale of her home had come and gone, and remarked to us that we inform people that they better be ready to move if they intend to utilize this effective Black Sect feng shui cure.

James and Helen Jay are internationally recognized experts in BTB Feng Shui and traditional feng shui. They lead feng shui intensive tours to China twice yearly, and conduct practitioner training seminars at their teaching center in Nevada City, California. They own **Feng Shui Designs**, *an outlet for quality feng shui products. Helen and James may be contacted at: www.fsdi.com **or call 1-800-551-2482 (530) 470-9215. Email:james@fengshuidesigns.com.***

My favorite Feng Shui real estate success story occurred in less than 48 hours and I never saw the property! Chatting before dance class, a fellow student danced over and said, "Oh, you do Feng Shui," and mentioned that she was financially desperate to rent one of her properties.

Five minutes to warm up, I briefly mentioned that she should make sure that she clean out the clutter and tidy up her SE (wealth) and NW (helpful people) areas of the space she was living in as well as do a mental chi (or energy) clearing out the rental property. With the excellent Feng Shui knowledge that Holly has shared, I am confident that you already know why it is vital to clean up your home first!

The purpose of the chi clearing is to remove the energy of the old occupants to welcome and invite new tenants to enter. To apply a simple analogy: A glass will hold a limited amount of liquid; once emptied, it can be refilled. When there is old energy in an environment, there is no room for new. Clear out the old chi and the space becomes more readily available, thus easier to rent (sell)!

Some may call the chi-clearing process a visualization, meditation, or ceremony. But for those who find those words foreign, it is really quite simple. All you need to do is spend a few minutes of concentrated focus (leaving all other thoughts for another time) with specific intention. Ask the space to release the energy of the old occupants and to be energetically empty. Thank the space for its previous support and invite it to be receptive to the new occupants.

When you have twenty or so minutes of uninterrupted quiet time (yes, turn off your cell phone!), take slow, deep breaths and focus on loving and protective thoughts. Visualize these thoughts as a warm, protective light that fills your body as if it were a balloon. For those familiar with meditation, use whatever techniques you prefer.

If you'd like to include assistance from your spiritual belief system, please do. Incorporate music, incense, sage, candles, or (my favorite) essential oils — any of these will help you to focus. I like to fill my heart, mind, and body with silver Mother Earth energy and gold energy from Father Sun. Then I fill the space with welcoming cinnamon, tangerine, and pine fragrances that incorporate the heaven and earth essence of Feng Shui.

Continue to expand your chi beyond the porosity of your body as if it were a balloon. Now your body is enveloped in this good energy that is filled with your personal power and loving intention. Extend your energy to occupy every nook and cranny of the property as you push out the energy of the previous tenants. Push this visualization of your own essence through the porous walls of the space squeezing out all unwanted energy.

Now here is the critical part. In your mind's eye, with the same concentrated focus, ask the space if it is clear and will it welcome new occupants. If your mind and heart are receptive, your intuition (and we all have it) will hear it say "YES." Repeat the process until you know that the home is ready to welcome its new family. When you are sure there is no more of the old tenant's chi and the space is clear, thank the home and quickly draw your energy back into your body through all the areas of the house. Reduce the balloon by concentrating it smaller and more densely. Bring it back to your heart and mind. Thank any loving assistance that you asked to assist you. As you leave the space, be ready to greet your day with the joy of matching people to their homes. Have Fun! Out with the old, in with the new! At the next class, my dance partner sashayed up to me grinning from ear to ear, thrilled that *the new tenant was moving in over the weekend!*

While there are many, many important and technical overlays or layers to consider in a Feng Shui evaluation, there are many circumstances that validate the essential power of thought and intention. When you purposefully set out to accomplish a task, allowing thought to create form, whatever your positive intention, the channel of receptivity opens and welcomes the opportunity for that possibility.

*Jami Lin is a professional interior designer with over 25 years of experience. As an internationally renowned lecturer, author, and consultant, Jami is recognized for her depth of knowledge in all aspects of feng shui, including Flying Star, Eight mansions, Compass and Black Sect traditions, humanitarian, psychological and intuitive. She is the originator of **Feng Shui Earth Design.**™ Visit www.jamilin.com for Jami's FREE feng shui readings and greetings, information, Q & A chat room, feng shui video clip, decorative feng shui products, and specials on her books/videos. To contact her: info@jamilin.com, Telephone: 305-756-6426, fax: 305-751-9995, POB 530725, Miami Shores, FL 33153.*

From Kathy Mann, feng shui consultant and teacher living in Tampa, Florida:

It has been my great fortune to assist many clients with the quick sale of their homes and businesses using feng shui knowledge. I especially wish to thank all my teachers, especially H.H. Grandmaster Lin Yun, for their assistance in my training over the years. Whenever called to do feng shui for real estate, I make it clear to the seller that two things must be in place for the sale to be smooth: the asking price must be reasonable for the current market and the owners have no strong emotional attachments to the home.

A couple called to have me help them sell their two bedroom townhouse that had been on the market for several months. The offers they had received were nowhere close to their asking price. They assured me their price was realistic and that they were emotionally ready to sell.

As I approached their street, there were no other homes for sale in the neighborhood and their property backed up to a beautiful wooded area; all good feng shui. What distinguished each house were the minor touches that owners were able to make within each front gate. At their entryway, I had to duck to avoid being hit with foliage because landscaping was overgrown and obstructed the path.

Their front door was angled and hidden from the street by the protruding garage. Additionally, large potted plants surrounding the door restricted the entry space. When I walked in, there was clutter in almost every direction, a floral arrangement on a pedestal was very close to the door, and there was a clear view of the stove from the entry. There was some attractive artwork that moved the chi up the stairs, however you could see the cluttered office at the landing. The master bedroom was nice but had a broken vanity mirror that blocked the path into the room. The wealth area of the bedroom contained a cluttered bookcase with a dried flower arrangement that symbolized dead chi.

To facilitate a good feng shui sale and get the fair market value, I explained why the front path and the foliage needed to be trimmed back for the chi to make its way easily to their door. Since there were too many plants near the front door giving a tight feeling in the area, we opened up the space leaving the two nicest ones.

In the interior, we moved the pedestal and floral arrangement opening up the space for better energy flow. The various areas of clutter were cleared, several of the pictures were re-arranged up the stairs, and the broken vanity mirror was removed. The owners completed most of these minor changes within minutes, and the positive impact could be felt immediately.

I gave them several more tips about aromatherapy to use when the house was being shown. Lastly, I shared with them the Real Estate Cure (as explained in Appendix C). The owners followed my instructions carefully the following Saturday morning. On Sunday, less than one week from my being there, an offer was made in the exact amount the sellers had requested during our consultation. The deal closed several weeks later.

Feng shui works regardless of location, or if a home is vacant or occupied. The key points are: a home's feng shui curb appeal, the first impression, front door chi, sincerity and intention of the owners, as well as the condition of the wealth and helpful people areas. The sellers need to make these necessary adjustments and know that the new owners are right around the corner.

*Kathy Mann operates **Feng Shui Creations**, of Tampa, Florida, specializing in both on-site and telephone feng shui consultations. She speaks professionally for conventions and teaches basic information to advanced training seminars nationally. Kathy can be reached at (813) 831-0263, or via the web: www.fengshui108.com.*

From Julie, a private homeowner living happily with her husband in San Luis Obispo, California:

John and I had lived in our house near the coast in Los Angeles for 10 years and decided it was time to sell; we wanted to retire to a smaller community. We are both from the Midwest, and I consider myself a bit of a skeptic when it comes to using something like feng shui to help sell our house.

But we really wanted to sell, despite the fact that it was a difficult real estate market. Knowing that we were going to need all the help we could get, I remembered some tips in the feng shui column in the *LA Times* that I had been reading for the past several months. Deciding anything was worth a try, John and I took matters into our own hands and followed the feng shui advice.

First we cleared out everything we absolutely didn't need and took 22 loads to the thrift store. Then we rented a storage unit to move out some of the bulkier furniture that we had accumulated over the years. Our overstuffed house was looking better already.

We really liked our real estate agent, Al, who suggested that we paint the weathered facia trim on the outside, and the tired-looking interior before we officially put the house on the market. We painted the dated dark kitchen white, including the cupboards, and re-finished the worn wood floors in the dining room. Yes, this required hard work to say the least, but now our house was looking great.

Continuing to follow the feng shui column's advice, I put brightly colored bowls of blooming flowers at each side of the front door, and placed a good number of lush plants throughout the house. I also installed a tabletop fountain in the southeast (the feng shui Wealth area) that I let run 24 hours a day. My skepticism was still there, but I had to admit the house felt wonderful, and I loved the fountain.

Our home had what real estate agents call character... a buyer would either love it or hate it. As we were preparing the last details, Al telephoned saying an agent in his office had a hot prospect who insisted on seeing the house as soon as possible. The broker caravan was scheduled for Wednesday, and the first open house was to be on Saturday. Our home wasn't even in the MLS system yet!

Before the buyer was due to come over, I grabbed the dogs and left. 45 minutes later Al called saying he had an offer on our house from the hot prospect... very close to our asking price with no contingencies. John and I signed the contract, but decided since the buyer's wife was out of town and hadn't seen the house, we should still have the broker caravan and open house anyway.

To make a long story short, when the wife came to see the house, again I grabbed the dogs and left. She loved it, and we closed escrow 30 days after the offer was made. John and I took off in our motor home to wait until when we could move into our wonderful retirement house in San Luis Obispo, still amazed that our property sold so fast in a slow market.

Was it feng shui that helped our house sell? I honestly don't know. However I do know that all the things we did according to the feng shui tips from the *LA Times* certainly didn't hurt.

Julie

Postscript: This past holiday season, John and I received a Christmas postcard from the buyers of our Los Angeles home saying how much they loved the house, and how grateful they are that they are there. They have a fountain too, and it runs all the time.

226

Appendix F:
The Life of an Escrow

Key:
Functions in ***bold italics*** indicate responsibilities of Title/Escrow company.
Functions in normal print indicate responsibilities of real estate agents.

The offer and acceptance

Initiate escrow with escrow officer.

Open escrow file and order title search.
Prepare escrow instructions.

Receive and review escrow instructions.
Originate new financing, order reports
(if requested). Advise buyer of obtaining fire
insurance policy.

Obtain signatures of buyers and sellers.

Review title report and resolve any apparent
title problems.

Request demands from beneficiaries
and other lien holders.

Advise escrow holder of loan
approval and fire insurance.

Verify anticipated closing
date with escrow holder.

Receive demands, termite inspection,
and other documents to extinguish obligations
of seller.

Receive new loan documents, fire insurance,
and secondary financing requirements.

Verify terms with listing
and selling agents.

Receive fully executed instructions, document
buyer funds, and review file to determine all
conditions have been met.

Request loan funds and verify any checks
deposited for buyer's account.

Update title information and record pertinent
documents. Proceed to close.

Prepare closing statements. Disburse all
proceeds and forward to interested parties.

Courtesy of

CUESTA TITLE

Glossary of Real Estate Terms

agency

term used to indicate the type of professional, fiduciary relationship that exists between buyers and sellers and their respective real estate agents

close of escrow

day on which the property is recorded at the county recorder's office in the new buyer's name and becomes part of public record. This is your goal!

closing costs

various fees associated with closing the escrow. Buyer and seller each have their respective costs to pay including, but not limited to title search, loan transfer, recording, and natural hazard disclosure searches.

CMA

competitive market analysis, performed by a real estate agent showing what price would be most appropriate for any given home in the current market based on sales of similar homes during the previous six months

contingency

serious condition imposed upon a contract, usually by the buyer, which, if not fulfilled or waived, can cause the sale to cancel

commission

a negotiable fee paid to a real estate broker for services performed in the buying or selling of real estate. Paid from seller's proceeds at close of escrow.

counter offer	offer subsequent to an original offer to purchase by a buyer. There may be more than one counter offer.
curb appeal	condition of a property as seen from the street. Usually has *significant* impact on a prospective buyer either for better or worse.
disclosure	responsibility of a seller to state in writing, anything of a material nature that they are aware of regarding the property they are selling. The responsibility for complete disclosure also applies to the agent representing the seller.
discovery period	time limit a buyer has to complete all their investigations regarding a property they are buying. This time frame is stated in the contract and binds all parties.
equity	value of a property after all fees, loans, liens, and commissions are paid
earnest money deposit	initial monetary amount paid by the buyer when submitting an offer to purchase real estate
escrow	neutral third party that assists a buyer and a seller with all the necessary documentation in the process of selling real estate
escrow fees	technically only the cost paid to the escrow company for their services; usually paid in equal amounts by the buyer and seller at close of escrow.

	Sometimes this term is used to refer to *all* the costs in connection with closing an escrow
escrow instructions	documentation of the purchase contract agreed to between buyer and seller
fiduciary	relationship of loyalty that legally exists between an agent and their principal (a buyer or seller)
final walk through	prior to close of escrow, the buyer and their agent will have a final inspection of the property. This usually takes place during the last week of escrow.
FSBO	*(pronounced fizz-bo)* For Sale by Owner
gift down payment	portion of the cash down payment coming from the buyer which has been *gifted* to them from a third party. A lender will usually require a written explanation from the giver that this money is *without strings*.
grant deed	legal document signed by the seller passing ownership to the new buyer which should be recorded
home inspection	thorough inspection made during escrow to obtain an understanding of the structural and mechanical aspects of a structure, the results of which are in report form; usually performed by a professional home inspector. Can be ordered by either a buyer or seller.

home warranty	one year insurance plan providing coverage for a majority of the mechanical aspects of a property
information flyers	usually provided by a listing agent and placed in a box or container on the real estate sign giving details about a property for sale; very helpful to buyers and selling agents!
lender	bank, savings & loan, mortgage banker, or mortgage broker who loans the buyer sufficient funds to purchase property
lien	(*pronounced leen*) monetary amount recorded against a property. This could be the result of a bill left unpaid or a disagreement with a contractor. Escrow cannot close until liens are paid or cleared from title.
listing	written agreement between a seller and a listing real estate broker authorizing the broker to offer the property for sale on behalf of the seller
lockbox	device, provided by a real estate agent, able to hold a key to the premises in a secure manner, allowing only authorized persons to enter
MLS	abbreviation for *Multiple Listing Service;* local real estate organization that provides detailed information to member brokers and agents, usually in book format and also by on-line data base

mortgage	usually refers to the loan obtained by the buyer and secured by a piece of real estate. In most states this is called a Note and Deed of Trust.
mortgage banker	a lender that is in control of the final funding; this is *the bank* and needs no other underwriting from outside sources. (Note: there is a difference between a mortgage *broker* and a mortgage *banker.*)
mortgage broker	broker that works with many different lending institutions, similar to an insurance broker, who places a loan with the best source they can find. *They are not in control of final funding*, but rather act as a middle-man to place a loan on behalf of their buyer client.
real estate agent	individual licensed to practice and derive compensation for, the buying and selling of real estate; must have their license under a real estate broker
real estate broker	individual who has passed a broker examination in the state in which they carry on business; an employer of real estate agents. Bears legal and professional responsibility for the actions of agents who work under the broker's real estate license.
REALTOR®	designation given to members of the National Association of REALTORS®, which holds its members to a strict

professional code of ethics in assisting buyers and sellers with real estate

red flag   condition of the property that warns a buyer or agent that a problem exists; for example, serious erosion, cracked foundation, or un-level flooring

title   manner in which real estate is legally held and recorded. It is very important to be clear about how title to property is taken; can have serious legal and estate consequences.

twin home   sometimes called a zero-lot-line-home; has a common wall down the center with each side having individual ownership

Glossary of Feng Shui Terms

arguing doors   doors which are awkwardly placed and when opened, bump into each other

bagua   ancient eight-sided energy template used in feng shui for mapping of the eight life sectors

bagua mirror   octagonal shaped device with a circular central mirror, always hung outside a building, often over the front door, to ward off sha chi coming from an external force such as a tall building or nearby freeway traffic

bau-biolgie   translated from German as "building of living things," this is a current movement that encourages the holistic, healing home. First developed in Germany, it has a strong environmental emphasis applied to both structures and the materials within buildings.

biting doors   doors which are unevenly aligned, as in a hallway or corridor

Black Tibetan Sect School

Brought to the West by H.H. Grand Master, Prof. Thomas Lin Yun several decades ago from China, BTS emphasizes transcendental or mystical cures. The setting of intention is considered to be the prime factor that activates beneficial chi. BTS combines Tibetan Tantric Buddhism, Taoist philosophy, and traditional Chinese methods, and is extremely popular in the United States.

Book of Changes	also known as the ***I Ching***, considered to be the oldest book of Chinese wisdom which emphasizes *right conduct of the superior man.* Still in widespread use today, both as a guide and an oracle.
chi	*(pronounced chee)* the cosmic breath of life; the energy which flows throughout the universe and permeates the land, people, spaces within buildings, giving the "life force" to all things
Chinese New Year	usually falls close to the first week in February on the Western calendar, and is named in cycles for the twelve celestial animals of the zodiac: Rat, Ox, Tiger, Hare, Dragon, Snake, Horse, Sheep, Monkey, Cock, Dog, Boar.
command position	the area in a room, farthest from the doorway, yet facing the door; a bed, desk chair, or any seating placed in this position provides the utmost visibility and security. Also referred to as the "power position"
Compass School	also called the *Fukien School,* school that applies feng shui principles according to directional orientation and relies on the use of the feng shui compass, or luo-pan. Compass School feng shui lays stress on the eight trigrams of the *I Ching*, the Heavenly Stems, the Earthly Branches, and the Constellations. Originating approximately 960 A.D., Compass School emphasizes the most auspicious front door placement of a home be facing South.
crystals	considered in feng shui to be strong earth energy enhancers , diffusers, and deflectors of sha chi.

Both natural and man-made crystals are effective and are used for different purposes.

Destructive Cycle of Elements

(Also called the Controlling Cycle) used in both interior and exterior design. This cycle of elements acts to "balance or control" one another. Metal cuts wood, wood displaces earth, earth dams water, water extinguishes fire, fire burns wood.

dragon lines

a Chinese geomancer's description of pathways of energetic power very similar to the ley lines described by Alfred Watkins

Earthly Branches

the twelve Earthly Branches give specific information about time and place on the feng shui compass. Associated with location of earth (dragon) chi, they also indicate the twelve double-hour divisions of the day, as well as the twelve months of the year. (Skinner, p.79)

feng shui

(pronounced fung schway) translated from the Chinese means wind and water. The ancient art/design science of harmony and balance within an environment.

Five Elements

fire, earth, metal, water, and wood, which, according to ancient Chinese tradition, comprises all life on earth, called *wu-hsing* in Chinese.

Form School

the original school of feng shui which developed in the south of China over four thousand years ago

geomancy

a former term for feng shui, inappropriately used today. More correctly, geomancy relates to an Arab form of divination. (Skinner, p. xi)

Heavenly Stems	the ten Heavenly Stems mark the position of the constellations at the beginning of the New Year. Sometimes referred to as containing water, similar to our western term the Milky Way. (Skinner, p.77)
hexagrams	the sixty-four combinations of trigrams from the *I Ching*
I Ching	*(pronounced Ee Ching)* also called ***The Book of Changes***; said to be the oldest source of Chinese right conduct, and contains the sixty-four hexagrams on which, and among other things, feng shui is based
intention, setting of	the most powerful and important aspect of deriving benefits from feng shui, and especially emphasized in the Black Tibetan Sect School
intuitive school	not a specific *school* as such, intuitive feng shui is practiced instinctively by artists, interior designers, architects, and lay persons with natural artistic talent
Kan-yu	*(pronounced kan-yoo)* ancient term for early form of feng shui
Later Heaven sequence	
	arrangement of the bagua trigrams according to better suit the "homes of the living" as opposed to the "homes of the dead" or graves in early feng shui practice
ley lines	term coined by Alfred Watkins, a British scientist and photographer, referring to the pattern of energetic connection between ancient sacred sites such as Stonehenge and Salisbury Cathedral. Not restricted to England, ley lines are similar to energetic pathways within a

238

	world-wide mapping system and produce positive vortexes of energy. Sedona, Arizona is said to be an example of ley lines and vortex power.
Life Sectors	the eight areas of living which are addressed as life sectors within feng shui: Career, Wisdom & Knowledge, Family & Elders, Wealth & Abundance, Fame & Reputation, Love & Relationships, Children & Creativity, Helpful People & Travel (see Appendices A & B)
luo pan	*(pronounced lo pan)* the traditional feng shui compass used by practitioners that contains concentric rings of Chinese words and symbols showing references required for Compass School analysis of a home, office, or building site
Magic Square (Lo Shu)	the ancient mathematical construct of nine numbers arranged in three rows, so that when added in any direction, totals fifteen
mantra	typically "O Ma Ni Pad Me Hum" a holy and reverently spoken chant similar to a western prayer, such as the recitation of the Our Father. Spoken, preferably nine times when setting a feng shui intention
mirrors	said to be the "aspirin" of feng shui, and used as a solution for numerous design challenges and to deflect sha chi
mudra	*(pronounced moodra)* hand gesture which reinforces the intention set when putting a feng shui cure or remedy into place, such as folding

the hands together, fingers upright, as in a prayerful attitude

mundane   having to do with a physical or simple feng shui application or cure, such as painting a dark colored, heavy, overhead beam white in order to make it visually disappear

nine   considered to be a powerful number in feng shui, nine is the highest single digit. Often used in multiples, nine is used whenever possible, to enhance and empower a feng shui cure.

Nurturing Cycle of the Elements

used constantly in feng shui to balance the design elements within a room or space: Fire produces ash (Earth), Earth generates Metal (ore), Metal holds Water, Water nourishes Wood, Wood feeds Fire

Om ma ni pad me hum

Buddhist mantra known as "the six sacred words… Praise to the Jewel of the Lotus." The lotus flower traditionally brings forth its loveliest blossom amid the murkiest of waters. Such is enlightenment to the human condition. Also called the "mantra of compassion."

pa kua   *(pronounced pa kwa)* Also *pa qua*. Compass School spelling for bagua (see bagua), the energetic template used throughout feng shui practice. The eight trigrams of the *I Ching* arranged in the Later Heaven Sequence.

Production Cycle of Elements

fire produces earth, earth contains metal, metal holds water, water nourishes wood, and wood feeds fire. Each element in turn feeds or nourishes the next. Also referred to as the *nourishing*, or *generative* cycle.

Red Envelope Tradition

Prior to any mystical feng shui remedy or solution being given from one person to another, the receiver gives the teacher a red envelope (or multiples of nine red envelopes) containing something of value. This tradition is considered extremely important, reflecting the pure intention of both giver and receiver of the cure. Following the Tradition of the Red Envelope shows the respect of the student, honors the work performed, and protects the positive chi of the giver.

remedies

interchangeable with solutions and cures

ru-shr

(pronounced roo-schur) logical feng shui cures; that which is easily used and understood

secret arrow

a design feature which has an intimidating influence over another, similar to a finger being pointed at you. Secret arrows in feng shui, send negative energy toward a structure or interior space, and are to be avoided or mitigated whenever possible.

sha (chi)

literally noxious vapor, the opposite of beneficial chi. Negative energy emanating from pointed corners, taller neighboring structures, power poles, nearby roof lines

shui

(pronounced schway) water or watercourse such as river, stream, or lake

solutions

feng shui remedies, a few examples of which are mirrors, wind chimes, or crystals. Solutions

Tai Chi *(pronounced tie chee)* the central area of the Bagua depicted by the Yin-Yang symbol, which represents overall well-being, and perfect balance of the specific environment under consideration. Considered to be the harmonious goal of feng shui design, and a power center within a specific space.

talismans Chinese mystical written blessings, often used by doorways, and when giving gifts. Used to ward off evil spirits, negative energy of all kinds, and to invoke the protective aspects of Heaven.

Taoism *(pronounced Daoism),* a philosophy associated with Tao, "the way," and is one of the original components of feng shui from ancient times. Actively practiced today, Taoism holds that beauty found in Nature is the ideal example of perfection.

three reinforcements

considered fundamental to the setting of intentions in feng shui practice: the mystical ingredients of using the **body**, as in a prayer-like hand gesture; the **mind**, as the intention or goal is powerfully visualized; the **speech**, by voicing aloud the prayer or mantra

ti li *(pronounced tee-lee)* name for feng shui in classical Chinese sources, translated as "land patterns" or in more modern times "geography" (Skinner, p. xi)

transcendental	referring to a more mystical or spiritual aspect of feng shui
trigrams	associated with the *I Ching, or Book of Changes*, the eight combinations of three solid or broken lines, one above the other, which represent various qualities or elements helpful to understanding the vicissitudes of life. By combining the trigrams in all their possible variations, the sixty-four hexagrams of the *I Ching* are produced.
wind chime	energy enhancer that employs movement and often sound. Used frequently in feng shui, both indoors and outside to empower or raise the chi in a particular spot.
yang	male or aggressive energy, associated with the source of power of Heaven
yi	the more transcendental or spiritual side of feng shui, the power of the spirit, will, and mind, concerned especially with the setting of intention to bring about specific desired results
yin	female or passive energy, associated with the receptive element of Earth

Bibliography

Books:

Alexander, Christopher. *A Pattern Language*. Oxford University Press. 1979.

---. *A Timeless Way of Building.* Oxford University Press. 1979.

Alexander, Jane. *Spirit of the Home*. Watson-Guptill. 2000.

Alvarez, Juan M., *Feng Shui – The Harmony of Life.* Fairy's Ring, 1998.

Bruss, Robert J. *The Robert Bruss Home Buyer's Workbook*. Tribune Publishing, 1991.

---. *The Smart Investor's Guide to Real Estate: Big Profits from Small Investments*. Crown Publishers, 1985.

---. *Effective Real Estate Investing*. Crown Publishers, 1985.

Collins, Terah Kathryn. *The Western Guide to Feng Shui*. Hay House, Inc., 1996.

---. *Home Design with Feng Shui A-Z*. Hay House, Inc. 1999.

Cox, Kathleen. *Vastu Living – Creating a Home for the Soul*. Marlowe & Co. 2000.

Eitel, Ernest J. *Feng Shui*. Graham Brash, Ltd. 1985.

Irwin, Robert. *Tips & Traps When Selling a Home*. McGraw-Hill. 1996.

---. *Tips and Traps When Negotiating Real Estate.* McGraw-Hill. 1997.

Kennedy, David Daniel. *Feng Shui Tips for a Better Life*. Webcom Limited. 1998.

Kingston, Karen. *Creating Sacred Space with Feng Shui*. Broadway Books. 1996.

Lin, Jami. *Feng Shui Today-Earth Design, the Added Dimension.* Earth Design Inc. 1995.

---. *The Essence of Feng Shui.* Hay House, Inc. 1998.

---. *The Feng Shui Anthology.* Earth Design, Inc. 1997.

Linn, Denise. *Feng Shui for the Soul,* Hay House. 1999.

---. *Sacred Space, Clearing & Enhancing the Energy of Your Home.* Ballantine Books. 1995.

Mann, T.A. *Sacred Architecture*. Element. 1993.

Minter, Sue. *The Healing Garden.* Charles E. Tuttle Co., Inc. 1995.

Post, Steven. *The Modern Book of Feng Shui.* Byron Press Book. 1998.

Rossbach, Sarah. *Interior Design with Feng Shui.* Penguin Books, Inc. 1987

---. *Feng Shui – The Chinese Art of Placement.* E.P. Dutton. 1983.

Rossbach, Sarah & Master Lin Yun. *Feng Shui Design, The Art of Creating Harmony for Interiors, Landscape and Architecture.* Viking Press. 1998.

---. *Living Color,* Kodansha America, 1994.

SantoPietro, Nancy. *Harmony by Design.* Perigree Books, 1996.

Skinner, Stephen. *The Living Earth Manual of Feng-Shui.* Penguin-Arkana. 1982.

---. *Feng Shui,* Paragon, 1997.

Spear, William. *Feng Shui Made Easy.* Harper Collins. 1995.

Thompson, Angel. *Feng Shui,* St. Martin's Griffin. 1996.

Too, Lillian. *Lillian Too's Basic Feng Shui.* Oriental Publications. 1997.

---. *The Fundamentals of Feng Shui,* Element Books. 1999.

---. *The Complete Illustrated Guide to Feng Shui.* Element Books, Ltd. 1996.

---. *The Complete Illustrated Guide to Feng Shui for Gardens.* Barnes & Noble.1998.

Trevelyan, Joanna, *Holistic Home.* Sterling, 1998.

Periodicals:

Feng Shui for Modern Living, Stephen Skinner, Editor. London.

The Feng Shui Journal, James Moser, Editor. San Diego, CA

Natural Home Magazine, Laurel Lund, Editor. Published Bi-monthly.

Los Angeles Times, Los Angeles, CA

Index

Page numbers in italics indicate illustrations, checklists, etc.

250

plants
    possibility of damage by
        termite treatment,
        189-190
    use of, 26, 70, 79, 82, 84-
        85, 103, 108-109,
        120
porches, 80, 82, 83, *88-89*,
    119-120, *121-122*
potpourri, 71
Production cycle of elements,
    240
purple, 211

R

real estate agent, 156, 233
    appointments, 130-131
    commissions, 149-153
    interviewing, 146-149, *147*
    length of listing, 155
    lockbox versus
        appointment, 153-
        154
    selection of, 143-146, *144-
        145*
    services of, *141-142*
real estate terms, 229-234
red, 211
    as front door color, 94
red envelope, tradition of, 208-
    210, 241
red phoenix bird, 35, *36*
Relationships position, 69, *204,
    205*
right of rescission, 158, 163
ru-shr, 241

S

secret arrow, 241
Seller's Net Cost Sheet, 150
Seller's Transfer Disclosure
    form, 163
    See also disclosure
selling your home
    as-is sales, 161-164
    setting the stage, 128-129
    showing, 128-134, *135-
        136*
    talking directly to buyers,
        128-130, 131-132
    without an agent, 137-140
    See also real estate agent
seven, 214
sha chi (killing breath), 51-53,
    88, 207, 235, 236, 239,
    241
shoes, wearing indoors, 95
shui, 241
six, 214
skylights, 27, 92
sliding doors, 108-109
smoking odors, eliminating,
    71-72
solutions (remedies)
    See feng shui remedies
space, inappropriate use of, 114
spiral stairways, 108
stairways, 107-108
    entries and, 107
    spiral, 108
storage
    rented units, 115
    sheds, 119

About Holly Ziegler

Holly Ziegler has been exploring the many aspects of houses and homes since childhood. Her father was an architect and through his influence, her courses in college emphasized architectural design and artistic approaches to the home environment. She earned her Bachelor's degree in Art and Home Economics and her Master's in Education from California Polytechnic University. Holly is the proud mother of two children.

Since 1976, Holly is credited as being one of the most successful real estate brokers on California's Central Coast, and is a consistent multi-million dollar seller. With hundreds of satisfied clients, she frequently consults on successfully marketing a residence or business.

With her experience in homes, architecture, and design, the ancient oriental art of feng shui has been a natural progression in Holly's work. She has traveled worldwide and studied feng shui intensively with recognized masters in China and the United States.

Currently she conducts workshops, teaches numerous seminars, and instructs feng shui courses at local colleges.

*Holly co-founded the **Feng Shui Association of the Central Coast** and writes feng shui columns for San Luis Obispo's **The Information Press**. Across the nation, Holly is a favorite on many radio and television talk shows. In addition to her current book, which is the first in a series of real estate and feng shui texts, she will be producing several Feng Shui in Real Estate videos that will soon be available through Dragon Chi™ Publications.*

Holly's much-in-demand feng shui consultations are available for both residential and commercial properties. Helping others to buy and sell their homes, and achieving harmony, balance, and overall well-being within their personal environments is her delight.

**The Open Door
Feng Shui Consulting**
*P.O. Box 1036 • Arroyo Grande, CA 93421
1 (866) 372-4660
e-mail: Holly@RealEstate-FengShui.com
and visit her website: www.RealEstate-FengShui.com*

Easy Order Form

Sell Your Home FASTER with Feng Shui
Ancient Wisdom to Expedite the Sale of Real Estate

Learn the secrets and solutions to sell your home from feng shui expert, and multi-million dollar real estate broker, Holly Ziegler.

Holly has studied feng shui intensively on site in China, and is a highly sought after speaker, instructor, workshop leader, and feng shui consultant on the California Central Coast. She combines the wisdom of this ancient design-science with two decades of successfully listing and selling millions of dollars of real estate.

Among the professional tips Holly shares…

How to:

- ✓ **stage your home to maximize every showing**

- ✓ **avoid common seller's mistakes and pitfalls**

- ✓ **handle home inspections, termite reports, and the escrow process**

- ✓ **…much, much more**

Put the "Real Estate Chi" Guru on YOUR Team!

(Turn page for order forms.)

Easy Order Form

Sell Your Home FASTER with Feng Shui

Please Send:

_____ copies of *Sell Your Home FASTER with Feng Shui* @ $16.95

Subtotal $_____

U.S. shipping $4.50 (1-5 books) $_____

California residents, add 7.25% tax $_____

Total order $_____

Ship to _____

Address _____

City _____ State _____ Zip _____

Phone or e-mail _____
(if we have questions or need more information to promptly fill your order)

Order online: **www.RealEstate-FengShui.com**

P.O. Box 1036 - Arroyo Grande, CA 93421
Toll-free (866) 372-4660
e-mail: Holly@RealEstate-FengShui.com

Consultations, seminars, and workshops, contact
Holly toll-free at (866) 372-4660

The best gift a seller could receive!

Easy Order Form

Sell Your Home FASTER with Feng Shui

Please Send:

_____ copies of *Sell Your Home FASTER with Feng Shui* @ $16.95

Subtotal $_____

U.S. shipping $4.50 (1-5 books) $_____

California residents, add 7.25% tax $_____

Total order $_____

Ship to _____

Address _____

City _____ State _____ Zip _____

Phone or e-mail _____
(if we have questions or need more information to promptly fill your order)

Order online: www.RealEstate-FengShui.com

P.O. Box 1036 - Arroyo Grande, CA 93421
Toll-free (866) 372-4660
e-mail: Holly@RealEstate-FengShui.com

Consultations, seminars, and workshops, contact
Holly toll-free at (866) 372-4660

The best gift a seller could receive!

Notes

Notes

Notes

Notes

Notes

Notes

Notes

Notes

Notes

Notes

Notes

Notes